My Dear Mr. M

LETTERS TO
G.B. MacMillan

FROM
L. M. Montgomery

EDITED BY
FRANCIS W. P. BOLGER
& ELIZABETH R. EPPERLY

Amanda

Toronto
OXFORD UNIVERSITY PRESS
1992

Oxford University Press, 70 Wynford Drive, Don Mills, Ontario
M3C 1J9

Toronto   Oxford   New York
Delhi   Bombay   Calcutta   Madras   Karachi   Petaling Jaya
Singapore   Hong Kong   Tokyo   Nairobi   Dar es Salaam
Cape Town   Melbourne   Auckland

and associated companies in
Berlin   Ibadan

Canadian Cataloguing in Publication Data
Montgomery, L. M. (Lucy Maud), 1874–1942
   My dear Mr. M.

Includes bibliographical references and index.
ISBN 0-19-540905-1

1. Montgomery, L. M. (Lucy Maud), 1874–1942 -
Correspondence.   2. MacMillan, George Boyd.
3. Novelists, Canadian (English) - 20th century -
Correspondence.* I. Bolger, Francis W. P., 1925-
II. Epperly, Elizabeth R.   III. Title.

PS8526.055Z545   C813'.52   C92-093108-1
PR9199.3.M6Z492   1992

My Dear Mr. M: Letters to G.B. Macmillan

OXFORD is a trademark of Oxford University Press
1 2 3 4 - 95 94 93 92
Printed in Canada by John Deyell

Contents

This book is dedicated to
Margaret Walsh Bolger
and
Elizabeth Rollins Larsen

Preface

Since the first publication of these selected letters in 1980, Montgomery scholarship has changed radically. No longer is L. M. Montgomery dismissed as a children's author who supposedly scribbled romances and formula fiction for girls. Now she is prized as Canada's most famous writer, who offers insightful fictional biographies of girls and women and wonderfully detailed accounts of Canadian rural life. Critics speak of her touching "the deepest places in the heart of childhood" and a "universal nerve" in her portraits of exuberant, independent spirits. The yearning, the oppressed, the beauty-loving, the young at heart find Montgomery's writing irresistible.

One of the major factors contributing to the change in the assessment of Montgomery is the publication of her journals under the capable co-editorship of Drs. Mary Rubio and Elizabeth Waterston. Montgomery kept a journal from the time she was small, recording events, impressions, and thoughts. She frequently copied from the journals into her letters and novels. Now that we have the journals, we can see what Montgomery chose to copy for MacMillan and what she created solely for him. In *My Dear Mr. M* we find a condensed form of the major events from the hundreds of pages of the diaries. Just exactly what was Montgomery able to confide to her slightly younger male pen-pal? A comparison of the journals and letters shows that she told him much.

When Lucy Maud Montgomery wrote to George Boyd MacMillan, she was talking to a kindred spirit who appreciated all of her thoughts and doings. Her letters to him are really an intimate autobiography, delivered in instalments. In a conversational voice she creates just for him, Maud Montgomery tells the aspiring writer from Scotland what she thinks about life, love, writing. Years before she was famous she was telling him all about her Cavendish activities; when she achieved world fame with *Anne of Green Gables* and eventually left Prince Edward Island to live as a minister's wife in Ontario, she continued to tell MacMillan how she felt about her everyday world as well as the greater world around. She kept secrets from her pen-friend but she also trusted him with her inmost thoughts.

L. M. Montgomery is always a good story teller and in the letters she gauges her audience sensitively, spinning out a long and rich narrative. It is obvious from the tenor of her letters to him that MacMillan was impressed and enthralled with the woman and the writer. And so are we.

Elizabeth R. Epperly
Francis W. P. Bolger
Charlottetown, P.E.I.
August 1991

Introduction

*"I wonder if, a hundred years or so after you and I
are dead someone will dig up our old letters and if so
will they create any furore."*
L. M. Montgomery to G. B. MacMillan
August 29, 1926

*Even though L. M. Montgomery's correspondence to George
Boyd MacMillan will not create "any furore," it does offer surprises. Their epistolary conversations over the thirty-nine-year
friendship range from the structure of the universe to the proper
method of caring for daffodils. They are kindred spirits and
share interests in literature, nature, gardening, cats, dreams,
and coincidences. To him, Maud Montgomery outlines the one
passionate romance of her life; with him she speculates on rein-
carnation and spiritualism. They vow early in the correspondence to be frank with each other; because she is true to this vow,
many of the letters in this volume make compelling reading.*

*The correspondence begins when Miriam Zieber of Philadel-
phia, an indefatigable if ungifted writer, decides to create an
exclusive literary circle. She corresponds with many writers,
among them Ephraim Weber of Alberta, G. B. MacMillan of
Scotland, and L. M. Montgomery of Prince Edward Island.
She puts the two men in touch with L. M. Montgomery: in
1902 Weber writes to L. M. Montgomery, and in 1903 Mac-
Millan writes to her. Miriam (Zieber) Watrous fades from the
scene, but the correspondences with MacMillan and Weber last
L. M. Montgomery's lifetime. The correspondence to MacMillan is intimate and revealing, and in this volume we reproduce
what we consider to be the best and most characteristic portions
of it.*

Since the twenty-two-year old G. B. MacMillan is himself an aspiring writer, serving as an apprentice with a local paper in Alloa, Scotland, much of the early correspondence deals with publishers and publishing. L. M. Montgomery *is twenty-nine years old when the correspondence begins (though she tells him she is twenty-six) and obviously feels that she is the old hand giving advice to the neophyte. She provides him with titles of receptive Canadian and American journals and indicates the types of manuscripts they prefer and the amount they pay. The lists disappear by 1905, and the advice eventually takes the form of periodic, friendly admonitions to get on with his book. In the early years of the correspondence, their relationship changes from professional camaraderie to friendship.*

Literature is an important bond between them throughout the years. The letters are filled with literary references and snippets of poetry. At Christmas they exchange books, and she is always captivated by his choice. Even when her health fails and her world seems to go sadly awry, she and MacMillan can share their love of reading.

In their early correspondence especially, both MacMillan and L. M. Montgomery are interested in love. She discusses the concept with detachment, patronizing him since she has experienced the emotion, and he has not. It is curious that she does not tell him of her engagement to Ewen Macdonald, and yet we find throughout the correspondence, even when their friendship has ripened, that she keeps a certain distance between MacMillan and her domestic life. She may tell him over the years of Macdonald's frequent illnesses, but not until the last letter in 1941 does she suggest the real horror of them.

She shares with MacMillan many of the other joys and burdens of her life. She delights in her two sons and quotes Stuart, the younger. On a less personal level, she is thrilled by motor cars, the talkies, and her own home movie camera. It is fascinating, though hardly satisfying, to see Anne of Green Gables *as a film. A visit from her friend, Nora Campbell, turns the prose of her letters to lyric. A visit to Prince Albert and the reunion with another friend, Laura Agnew, occasions rhapsody.*

Characteristically, L. M. Montgomery's depressions are as intense as her elations. She pours out to MacMillan her anguish over the campaigns of World War I, relating what she hopes are prophetic dreams of ultimate victory. At the end of the war her beloved friend and cousin, Fredericka Campbell, dies and the agony L. M. Montgomery suffers is frightening.

She mourns the deaths of her two P.E.I. cats, Daffy and Lucky. Daffy first and later Lucky are far more to her than pets—they are companions, friends. Since MacMillan also loves cats, she can reveal her heartbreak to him when Lucky, one of her most cherished links with P.E.I., dies.

During the course of her friendship with MacMillan, L. M. Montgomery changes from a confident and cheerful young woman to a disillusioned but courageous old woman. She is resilient throughout the Leaskdale and Norval years, despite numerous sorrows. After her retirement to "Journey's End" in Toronto, however, her health and spirits fail.

The common strand in every fibre of the correspondence, sustaining her in sorrowful times, supporting her devotion to beauty, is her love for Prince Edward Island. She returns from visits with a sense of wonder and describes the landscape to MacMillan in rapturous words. The extent of her emotional decline is apparent in the briefness of her note to MacMillan on her last visit home in 1939. Nineteen of her twenty novels (The Blue Castle is the exception) are set, wholly or in part, on Prince Edward Island; fifteen of these are written while she lives in "smug opulent Ontario." The Island is always her spiritual home.

L. M. Montgomery's letters are charming. They can be gloomy, even morbid, but they can also be arch, witty, warm. Above all, they are readable. They give insight into the character of one of Canada's best-known authors, revealing her personality and its changes as the thirty-nine-year friendship develops. The deliberate silences on some subjects are themselves provocative. We read the letters on different levels, seeing what she means for MacMillan to see, and appreciating what she reveals about herself inadvertently. And we do, of course, read the letters for themselves. On whatever level and for whatever reason we read them, we find that L. M. Montgomery, throughout, keeps her vow to MacMillan to make theirs a stimulating correspondence.

Acknowledgements

We would like to thank Dr. Stuart Macdonald for his kind permission to publish his mother's letters to George Boyd MacMillan. We would also like to thank Mollie Gillen, who discovered the letters to MacMillan and made excellent use of them in her biography of L.M. Montgomery. We thank Shirley Dillon, Ann Doiron Harding, and Barbara Mullaly for assistance in preparing the typescript. And to Mrs. Ruth Campbell, who provided pictures and information, we give special thanks.

Since the 1980 publication of these letters, Dr. Macdonald has died. We would like to thank the Montgomery Estate for permission to re-issue the letters in this edition.

The Years Before the Correspondence

Lucy Maud Montgomery spends thirty-four of the first thirty-seven years of her life on Prince Edward Island. She is born to Clara Woolner Macneill and Hugh John Montgomery on November 30, 1874, in Clifton (New London), P.E.I., and grows up in nearby Cavendish with her grandparents. When her mother dies of tuberculosis in 1876, her father wants to move to the West to begin a new life, and it is decided that the old Macneill homestead will be L. M.'s home.

Lucy Maud is a sensitive and precocious child and, though grateful to Alexander and Lucy Macneill, finds life with them difficult. Their narrowness and frequent insensitivity make her long for the time when she can join her father out West. He marries in 1887 and later settles in Prince Albert, Saskatchewan. He finally agrees to let her come in 1890, and L. M. makes the trip joyfully. But she underestimates both her love for Prince Edward Island and the problem of adjusting to her young stepmother. After one year she returns to Cavendish to live again with her grandparents.

She studies for the entrance examinations to Prince of Wales College and comes fifth on the Island. In 1893 she enters Prince of Wales, taking the second year of the two-year teacher's program, and earns a teacher's license in 1894.

L. M. has less than four years of independent life, three teaching school and one studying in college, before she is again living at the Macneill homestead. Her first school is in Bideford, P.E.I., where she teaches from 1894 to 1895. She then goes to Dalhousie University, as one of only twenty-nine female undergraduates, to take courses in English Literature. Her next school is in Belmont, Lot 16, and the last school, where she teaches from 1897 to 1898, is in Lower Bedeque.

On March 5, 1898, her grandfather dies, and L. M. Montgomery realizes that she must go back to Cavendish to be with her grandmother, who would otherwise have to leave the family homestead. By leaving Lower Bedeque she is not only giving up teaching, but she is also breaking off an intense relationship with Herman Leard, a young farmer whom she loves. For the next thirteen years, with only one nine-month break, she continues to care for her grandmother and to help run the Cavendish post office, which the Macneills had managed since 1870.

Throughout all the years—the early and the mature ones—in Cavendish, during one year out West, and during subsequent years at Prince of Wales College, at teaching posts, and at Dalhousie, L. M. Montgomery writes. After she returns to Cavendish, she begins to earn a comfortable living by her pen.

In 1901 she leaves for Halifax to spend eight months working on the newspaper the Daily Echo. *In 1903, one year after her return to Cavendish, she receives the first letter from George Boyd MacMillan.*

Notes on the Text

We mark omissions of more than three lines with a centred ellipsis (. . .). We preserve L. M. Montgomery's spelling and punctuation, although we make her use of single and double quotation marks consistent. (She is especially inconsistent with hyphens and capitals.) We keep footnotes to a minimum.

The Island Years
(letters from 1903 to 1911)

When L. M. Montgomery receives the first letter from G. B. MacMillan, she is coping with her domestic responsibilities and is struggling to establish herself as a poet and short-story writer with major American and Canadian magazines.

The early letters to MacMillan are cheerful. She shares with him her love of nature and her preoccupations with religion and love (even outlining her passionate relationship with Herman Leard), and yet is silent about two of the most important events of the Island years—the writing of Anne of Green Gables *and her engagement to the Reverend Ewen Macdonald.*

The August 1908 letter announces both the publication of Anne of Green Gables *and the completion of a second "Anne" book,* Anne of Avonlea. *During the next two years, as she tells MacMillan, she writes* The Story Girl *and expands "Una of the Garden" into* Kilmeny of the Orchard.

In March 1911 her grandmother dies. L. M. Montgomery moves to the home of her Uncle John and Aunt Annie Campbell of Park Corner, and there, on July 5, 1911, marries Ewen Macdonald. They leave for a honeymoon in the British Isles, where she meets G. B. MacMillan for the first and only time.

Cavendish, P.E.I.
Can.

Tuesday Evening
December 29, 1903

My dear Mr. McMillan:

I must ask your pardon for not answering your letter sooner. But I have been so busy over Xmas preparations that my correspondence was pushed entirely aside for the time being. Xmas is over and I am free once more so I shall try to pick up my dropped threads.

I shall be very pleased to carry on a literary correspondence with you and hope we can make it mutually helpful and interesting. I am particularly glad that you live in Scotland for I have no other correspondent there and think it is the most delightful and interesting land on earth. I am Canadian born and bred but my forefathers on both sides were from Scotland. Our family of Montgomery claim kinship with the Earls of Eglinton. My mother was a Macneill, which is even "Scotchier" still.

Like yourself, I will tell you a little about myself in order to enable you to visualize me a little bit and not leave you to think of me as only a vague intellectual proposition.

I am 26 years old and like yourself have been scribbling all my life. Six years ago I began to inflict my scribblings on a public that suffereth long and is kind. I have got on pretty well and make a comfortable living for one small girl by my pen besides finding a vast deal of pleasure in my work. Apart from my literary bent I am small, said to be very vivacious, am very fond of fun and good times generally. I write this because so many people have told me that from my writings they expected to see a tall, imposing looking girl with flashing black eyes and hair.

I don't know whether I call verse my specialty or not.

2

I know that I touch a far higher note in my verse than in prose. But I write much more prose than verse because there is a wider market for it, especially among the juvenile publications. In 1903 I have made $500 by writing of which less than $100 came from verse. I am glad you like my verse and shall be pleased to send you some of them in each letter if you would care to see them. I shall also be pleased to see anything and everything of yours. I have never attempted essay writing because I do not think I could do any thing in that line although I enjoy reading essays very much. My prose is all fiction—mostly short stories but I sold two serials this summer.

As you are trying to get into American journals I will give you all the "pointers" I can in any way. I have about 70 different periodicals on my list and will tell you about a few in each letter until I have gone through the list. Will put them on a separate sheet of paper.

I regret that I don't know of anybody who would wish to exchange American for British stamps. Miss Zieber[1] would be more likely to. I know very few writers but if I come across anyone looking for British stamps I will refer them to you.

Do you typewrite your Mss? I have done so for two years. I bought a good secondhand machine taught myself to manipulate it and type all my Ms. It has paid me, I think. Editors used to growl over my handwriting.

I sent you a couple of my "yarns" when I received your letter by way of letting you know that it had come to hand. Miss Zieber thinks my prose is poor and I do not claim any merit for it. But I am frankly in literature to make my living out of it. My prose sells and so I write it, although I prefer writing verse. I know that I can never be a really great writer. My aspiration is limited to this—I want to be a *good workman* in my chosen profession. I cannot be one of the masters but I hope to attain

1. See Introduction, p. vii.

to a recognized position among the everyday workers of my time. That is all I hope or expect.

I am interested in many things and *love living*. I have a camera and enjoy taking photos. I enclose a few unmounted "squeezes" of P.E.I. corners. I love *fancy-work, cats,* horses, pretty dresses and feminine things generally. Revel in books. Don't care for athletics but love out-of-doors. This is all a very egotistic strain but such can't be avoided in such a correspondence as this, especially at the start.

Whereabouts in Scotland is Alloa? Near Edinburgh? Don't roll your eyes over my ignorance?[sic] Remember I'm 2000 miles away and my ideas of Scottish geography are merely on broad general lines.

Well, I shall stop now for this time and shall look forward with pleasure to your next letter. I have a long list of correspondents but always try to answer each letter in turn.

Very fraternally yours,
L. M. Montgomery

The Congregationalist Boston, Mass. is a religious weekly which pays *very fair* prices for work. Two of the poems I enclose were published in it, "When I Go Home" and "Afterlight." For each I got $5 on publication. It accepts or rejects promptly and sends a complimentary copy. I have also sold it a number of juvenile stories of about 2000 words each for which it paid me $7 apiece. I should think it would be a good place for short 2000 word essays on interesting Scottish subjects but of course one can only tell this by trying it. It is thoroughly reliable.

The Messenger of The Sacred Heart, of the Apostleship of Prayer 27 West 16th St New York is a Catholic magazine. (*I* am a *blue* Presbyterian). It has bought several poems from me, paying five dollars apiece on acceptance. They were not religious. "The Poplars At The Gate" is one. They send complimentary copies. I think essays might stand a chance there if they were of the right kind. Of course they would have to contain nothing that would clash with Catholic readers.

The Youths' Companion, Boston, Mass. is the foremost paper of its class in America. Articles descriptive of Scottish life, traditions etc. ought to stand a chance. They pay from $8 to $15 for good verse on acceptance and send complimentary copy. This is *high price* for verse in America. "When The Fishing Boats Go Out" was published by them.

The Farm and Fireside, Springfield, Ohio, is an excellent paper of its class. Uses fiction and descriptive articles. Pays very fair prices—$14 for a story of 3000 words on acceptance and sends complimentary copy. Are prompt and reliable.

Cavendish, P.E.I.
Can.

Wednesday Evening
November 9, 1904

My dear Mr. McMillan:
I must use the same apology you did for my delay in answering your letter. Just after it came—Sept. 20—I left home for a month's visit and as I never can write letters away from home all correspondence was off tap until my return. I came home two weeks ago and since then have been so busy picking up dropped threads that I haven't got around to my letters before. It's a cold frosty night out with a skim of snow on the ground and a silvery new moon floating over the orchard in a sea of saffron yellow sky. I've just seen her over my right shoulder so am sure of good luck for a month.

So you have have gone into journalism![1] Good luck attend you. I know something of the life since, two years ago I spent nine months down in Halifax, N.S. on the staff of a daily paper[2] there. I was proof-reader, society editor and general handy man. I liked the life and the office atmosphere (metaphorically speaking: the literal atmosphere was generally too thick with cigar smoke to be exhilarating) very much; but I don't suppose it was exactly conducive to the best literary output. Still, I'm blessed with a faculty for being able to write pretty nearly anywhere. In my idle intervals in the office I could sit down among a constant crowd of comers and goers and gossiping reporters and write a story or poem, which was just as good as anything I had written in solitude. Still of course I prefer solitude for composition. Perhaps after you get accustomed to your new life you will learn this trick of self-isolation and will no longer have to lament the difficulty of composing under such circumstances.

·   ·   ·

I can't send you a picture of Cavendish, because such a thing doesn't exist. C. is a narrow farming settlement (for all the world like the "Dumtochty" of Ian McLaren's delightful stories in many of its characteristics) fronting on the Gulf of St. Lawrence. It is about three miles long and one wide. The narrow homestead farms front on the gulf and on each one is a house. As these are all strung along the three miles it's impossible to get more than one of them in the same picture. Some day I'll send you some of our C. homesteads when I get time to finish them. It is settled with the descendants of old Scotch (Lowland) emigrants—Macneills, Simpsons, Clarks,

1. MacMillan (1880-1952) has been a printer with the *Alloa Advertiser*, and, in 1904, becomes a reporter with the *Alloa Journal*.

2. She works on the Halifax *Daily Echo* from October, 1901, until June, 1902.

McKenzies, Robertsons, Stewarts—don't they smack of the heather. By the way have you ever been near Eglinton Castle, the habitat of the Montgomeries, earls of Eglinton. We claim descent from them.

The only snap I have to send this time is a little woodland haunt of mine. The little break in the path is a bridge over a brook. I go there nearly every day and love the spot.

You ask "do I think an innate discontent with one's environment is helpful to one's intellectual and spiritual development." Well, I would say it all depends on the discontent. Some discontents are ignoble. A petty, carping spirit of discontent, a sort of—this-place-isn't-good-enough-for-me-and-I'm-wasted-here affair cannot be helpful or uplifting and should certainly not be cultivated. But there is a certain discontent which I believe does ennoble because it impels us to try to improve our surroundings—to measure our happiness by what we can *put into* our environment, not by what we can *get out*. It would be foolish, because our environment may not be congenial in every respect, to accept it in a sort of resigned way, forcing a dull content because we cannot escape from it; and it would be equally foolish to antagonize people by posing as their superior in any way. We can't make over our environment to suit us but I do believe we can modify it very strongly—create just about us an environment of our own which must certainly leaven more or less our whole habitat.

· · ·

This evening I went for a walk—all alone but not a lonely one. I am sometimes lonely in the house or when walking with uncongenial company but I have never known a moment's loneliness in the woods and fields. I have rich, rare good company there. To-night in spite of the world's sadness I was not sad. I felt a conscious gladness as if there was in me something buoyant and immortal that rose above the decay and death of the year. The air was very frosty and clear. There were wonderful lakes of crimson and gold among the dark western hills. The fields were gray and quiescent, as if brooding over old joys and folding their arms about baby germs that must be kept safe for another spring.

The woods were very silent. The birches and maples were bare and gray but the firs were greener than ever and the frost had nipped them until the air about them was all resinous with their balsam. There is no sweeter odor than fir balsam distilled in the crucible of a frosty autumn night.

I went up through Lover's Lane—not the Lover's Lane of June, beautiful with maiden loveliness but beautiful with the beauty of a woman who has lived and wept bitter tears and wears her sorrow like a garment of praise.

A brook was laughing to itself in the hollow. Brooks are always in good spirits. They never do anything but laugh. It is infectious to hear them, those gay vagabonds of the valleys.

While I think of it I want to ask a favor of you. If it is too much trouble you need not grant it. We have a Literary Society here and I'm a member of the Entertainment Committee for the winter. One night in February we are going to have a "magazine" and I am "editor." Will you contribute a brief sketch, as brief as you like for it. Something descriptive of some interesting spot in Scotland would be good but you may write on the nebular hypothesis if you like. I shall be so much obliged if you only can for I've such a hard time getting enough material but I don't want to inconvenience you in any way.

.   .   .

Yours very faithfully,
L. M. Montgomery

Cavendish, P.E.I.
Can.

Monday Evening
June 5, 1905

My dear Mr. M.:
"What so fair as a day in June?" This has been one of its
fairest. The whole world seems abloom. As I sit here at
the window of my "den" I look down on a wide green
field lush with neatly sprung clover, a lane where I
know purple violets are growing thickly and an orchard
arrayed as if for a bridal in rose and snow. It is just good
to be alive in a world where there are Junes.

.   .   .

Oh, if you'll only send me a bit of Blarney Castle! *Please,
please*, do. I already see myself the proud possessor of it.
Altho' not exactly a piece of the immortal stone itself it
has been near enough it for some virtue to have leaked
down I'm sure.

.   .   .

I liked your friend's poems much—especially the Burns'
one. I'd like anything in praise of Burns I think—like an
old great grandfather of mine who said he'd "love a
weasel if it was named Nancy." Nancy was his wife's
name and thereby hangs a tale which, since it has come
into my mind, I'll write down for you to smile over.

Over a hundred and fifty years ago P.E.I. was not the
fair garden-like province it is to-day. It was unsettled
and thickly covered with woods. At that time there
flourished a certain Donald Montgomery who lived on
the eastern shore of Richmond Bay (see map). His most
intimate friend was a certain David Murray who lived at
Bedeque. From friends however they soon became

9

rivals. On the western shore of Richmond Bay lived a family by the name of Penman. They were United Empire Loyalists, who left America at the close of the War of Independence and came to Canada. They had been people of birth and wealth in the U.S. but having forfeited all their property were miserably poor. The two daughters, Nancy and Betsy, however, were so remarkably beautiful that they had lovers by the score. Among these Donald and David had both set their affections on the fair Nancy. It was a hot race between them and as Nancy was very impartial in her favors each came to believe that whoever got the chance or the courage to "pop" first would win the lady.

One cold winter day Donald—who kept bachelor's hall—was surprised by a call from David, on his way from Bedeque to the Penman's. Donald shrewdly suspected David's destination and purpose; so, under pretence of welcome he plied David with *whisky* until the latter lost his wit and confided to Donald that he was going over the bay to ask Nancy Penman to have him. Donald was a shrewd fellow: he kept on urging David to drink but took none himself. Finally David fell sound asleep. Then Donald took David's horse and sleigh and drove over the bay, reached the Penman's, proposed to and was accepted by Nancy. A storm coming up that night prevented David from pursuing. But early the next morning he came galloping over on Donald's colt, in a red-hot fury. But the birds had flown. Donald and Nancy were off—still with David's horse and sleigh—to be married and David was left lamenting. He stamped and swore and raised a fuss generally. Whereas Betsy, who had a will of her own and had long cherished a secret liking for this same David, spoke up in words that have come down as a family tradition, "I'm as good-looking a lass as Nan and *I'll* take you if you'll have me. Will you?"

David would—and did. And I've always heard it said that they were the happiest couple that ever lived. The daughter of Betsy and David, Anne Murray, married her first cousin, my grandfather, Senator Montgomery,[1] the son of Donald and Nancy. *Their* son was my father, so both Betsy and Nancy were my great-grandmothers. How is that for a bit of family romance?

. . .

Well, I must go now and weed my garden. It's a wonder I've been able to complete this letter without running out two or three times to sniff at the daffodils. Wish I could send you a whiff of their perfume.

Yours fraternally,
L. M. Montgomery

Cavendish, P.E.I.
Can.

Thursday Evening
August 23, 1905

My dear Mr. McMillan:
This is the fag end of a very doggy dog-day and was never meant for writing letters at all at all. But your bit of Blarney arrived to-day and I'm so full of gratitude for it that I must express it immediately before the "bouquet" thereof evaporates. Thanks devoutly. I can't tell you how pleased I am with it. My emotions are about on a par with my kitten's who caught his first mouse to-day!

Of course I've kissed the fragment believingly. Even although it isn't the Blarney Stone itself surely some virtue must have *leaked into it* during the years. I shall ex-

---

1. Senator Donald Montgomery (1808-1893).

pect an added smoothness of tongue henceforth—or perhaps it will show itself in my pen, which the gods permit!

Really, the word "Ayr" at the top of your last letter gave me a thrill! To think that I should be getting a letter from *Ayr*. Why, a blank sheet from there would be interesting! I'm a hero-worshipper and Burns—oh, what a magnificent creature he was! I've loved his poetry ever since I was a baby. A great many great poets appeal only or almost only to the intellect. Burns appeals to the heart and in this I think is the secret of his power. He makes his verses *live* with the richness of his own nature. You call him "the greatest exponent of *Scottish* life and character." Nay, leave out the "Scottish." Burns was of *humanity*, be it whatever nationality it will. He gave voice to the song that sings itself in *all* human hearts, whether in Scottish braes or Canadian prairies, and this is why we of this New World, remote from him in time and space, love him so well and so understandingly. Have you ever read the American poet Whittier's beautiful poem to Burns? If not, I will copy it and send to you.

.   .   .

I am sending you herewith a snapshot of our shore. The promontory is known as Cape Leforce and has a history. It was the scene of the first recorded murder on the Island: Long ago, as you know, P.E.I. then known as Island of Saint John belonged to France. In a war between England and France, about 17 and so on, French privateers haunted the St. Lawrence gulf and plundered the fisheries and commerce of the New England colonies. One of these, commanded by Captain Leforce, was very successful. Finally she anchored off our shore—which then, of course, was an uninhabited forest—and the captain and his mate landed on this cape to spend the night and divide their ill-gotten gains. They quarrelled over them and finally agreed to fight a duel on the cape at sunrise. But while the captain was marking off their respective positions the mate shot him dead through the heart. He was buried hastily on the cape and the mate sailed away. The grave has long since been washed away but my great-grandfather, I am told, remembered having seen it when a small boy. The cape has always been called Cape Leforce. It is one of our favorite bathing spots. Formerly that gap in the middle did not exist. The first little hole wore through when I was about ten years old. These soft red sandstone rocks crumble very rapidly. When I first saw it it was about big enough for a small dog to crawl through. I was a very adventurous kid and *I* tried to crawl through. As a result I got stuck. Couldn't go either backward or forward and there I was like a thread stuck thro' a needle's eye. I can't remember how I got out or why I am not there to this day.

Ten years from that time the little hole had enlarged to its present dimensions.

· · ·

You ask if I like music. Yes, I like music very much. That temperate sentence exactly expresses my attitude towards it. Music does *not* mean to me what it means to those who love it as you do. I regret this because no doubt I lose a great deal by reason of it. Yet I believe it is made up to me in other ways. *Color* is to me what *music* is to some. Everybody *likes* color; with me it is a passion. I revel in it. Last fall in town, attending a vaudeville performance I saw what was called a "Rainbow Dance"—a combination of colored lights thrown on a white-clad girl dancing. I never saw or imagined anything so utterly beautiful and *satisfying*. My emotions were exactly what you describe yours as being when listening to music. Everything you say of music I can say of color.

Hence I can understand what music means to you. On my table is a color effect of yellow California poppies that makes me dizzy with delight every time I look at it.

However, as I said, I like music very much, especially the homely, simple songs and ballads of any people. When I add, to crown all this, that I'm organist in our Presbyterian church here, you will understand—if you know anything about the tribulations of an organist with a country choir—that it's a miracle I don't utterly detest music!

. . .

I'm going back to the woods now to get some ferns. Want to come? I could make you useful opening gates and chasing cows. There are always cows back there and I'm always horribly scared of them! I want ferns to decorate the church for a lecture to-morrow night. I generally attend to the decorations, especially for Sunday services. To-night I've set my heart on having two enormous jars of palm ferns, one in each corner of the platform.

Good bye:—thanks for your postals, daisies, and last but not least your *charming* Burns' letter. (See if the Blarney stone isn't working already, Shure!)

Very sincerely yours
L. M. Montgomery

Cavendish, P.E.I.
Can.

Sunday Afternoon
December 3, 1905

My dear Mr. McMillan:

. . .

I was keenly interested in what you said in your letter about *living in the ideal*. Believe me it *is* possible—and thank God for it! It is possible to create our own world and live in it happily. *If* it were not I do not think I could exist at all—for the outward circumstances of my life are at present miserably circumscribed and carking—owing in great measure to poor old grandmama's[1] ways of age and rapidly increasing childishness—and I don't think I should have the courage or strength to endure them patiently if I could not escape from them into a world of the fancy. I think my experience in life in this respect has been very similar to your own. Perhaps it is the experience of all those sensitive souls
"By nature pitched too high,
By suffering plunged too low."
I was a lonely child. Orphaned by the early death of my mother I was brought up with my grandparents. In material respects they were good and kind to me and I am sincerely grateful to them. But in many respects they were unwise in their treatment of me, I think in all unprejudiced judgment. I was shut out from all social life, even such as this small country settlement could offer, and debarred from the companionship of other children and—in early youth—other young people. I had *no* companionship except that of books and solitary

---

1. Lucy Woolner Macneill (1824-1911).

15

rambles in wood and fields. This drove me in on myself and early forced me to construct for myself a world of fancy and imagination very different indeed from the world in which I lived, moved and had my outward being. In those days I had never read Emerson's famous passage about the ideal life: but I had found in very truth his "rose of joy" and its beauty and fragrance has sweetened my whole life until I thank God for living, even in a world where I have found so few souls that seemed to have much in common with mine. Do you know the passage? In case you do not I will quote it:—

"In the actual—this painful kingdom of time and chance—are Care, Canker and Sorrow: with thought, with the ideal, is immortal hilarity—the rose of joy; round it all the Muses sing."

Isn't that beautiful—and true?

Well, I grew up out of that strange, dreamy childhood of mine and went into the world of reality. I met with experiences that bruised my spirit—but they never harmed my ideal world. That was always mine to retreat into at will. I learned that that world and the real world clashed hopelessly and irreconcilably; and I learned to keep them apart so that the former might remain for me unspoiled. I learned to meet other people on their own ground since there seemed to be no meeting place on mine. I learned to hide the thoughts and dreams and fancies that had no place in the strife and clash of the market place. I found that it was useless to look for kindred souls in the multitude; one might stumble on such here and there, but as a rule it seemed to me that the majority of people lived for the things of time and sense alone and could not understand my other life. So I piped and danced to other people's piping—and held fast to my own soul as best I could. When it became necessary for me to return and stay here with grandmama I did so the less unwillingly because I knew I could possess my ideal world here as well as elsewhere—that

16

no matter what was missing outwardly I could find all in my own peculiar kingdom.

So don't despair because you think you have lost your ideal world. You haven't—it's there still—some day your feet will find their way back to it. Only don't hope you can ever fuse it with the real world, to the betterment of the latter. You can't—and it would spoil the ideal one if you could.

I think the majority of people *are* prosaic and unideal. I say this not in ignorance of the beautiful blossoms of unlooked for sentiment and romance which sometime spring up where we least expect to see them, in the homeliest lives. But, as a rule, I think the eyes of the multitude are holden and they don't see what we see— or dream we see. I have many friends here and else- where whom I love and with whom I often have pleas- ant times. But they are few indeed to whom I feel I can talk fully and freely out of my inmost "ego"—with whom I can feel that delightful "oneness" of sentiment and thought which hardly requires words to express it. It is the most chilling thing in the world to say some- thing to a person and be met by a blank wall of non- comprehension—a non-comprehension that cannot be hidden under any ready agreement in mere words, such as "That is very true"—or "Yes, indeed." So, as a rule, I am very careful to be shallow and conventional where depth and originality are wasted. When I get very des- perate I retreat into my realms of cloudland and hold delightful imaginary dialogues with the shadowy, con- genial shapes I meet there. It is not so satisfying as the *reality* of such might be but it is far better than to let one's soul slip down to sodden levels for lack of the stim- ulation which comes from the flash and meeting of other intellects.

That's enough of that, isn't it? I believe I would have made a good *preacher*. Only, when I got up in a pulpit, and saw facing me rows upon rows of dull, unresponsive, faces, unlit by a single flame breath of feeling, all my fine sentiments would probably collapse, like a punctured balloon and I would come down flat.

Re elocution:—well, I've always been accustomed to reciting in public and am mostly held to get along fairly well; but I never had any elocutionary training although I would have loved to. I could not, however, "speak" in public if I died for it. I can write a paper and read it; but to get up and say anything—horrors, I should die on the spot. We have a literary and debating club here and I just sit like a log while the others are talking eloquently. If I were to get up on my feet I wouldn't have an idea in my head. The worst of it is people won't believe I *can't*. They know I can write slickly and read well and they think it is just sheer obstinacy that I won't speak in a discussion. But I simply *cannot*. I would stammer and grope and make grammatical errors that would make the flesh creep on my bones in cold blooded thought afterwards.

.   .   .

By the way have you Simpsons in Alloa? Cavendish is full of them. My great-great-grandmother was a Simpson, born in Scotland.

No, I don't cycle. The craze for it has died out here. Four or five years ago *everybody* seemed to be cycling. I had to choose between a "bike" and a camera and choose [sic] the latter, so I never learned to ride a wheel before they went out of fashion. If they could run all winter I'd have one yet but as they can't negotiate snowdrifts I don't think I shall bother. They are fine for men, though, and you will probably get a lot of pleasure out of yours.

.   .   .

Yours cordially,
L. M. Montgomery

Cavendish, P. E. Island
Can.

Monday Evening:
March 19, 1906

My dear Mr. McMillan:
This is one of the days at the close of which I feel inclined to pat myself on the back! I have actually accomplished all the work which I planned to do when I got
up this morning. This doesn't happen more oftener
than once in a blue moon. Indeed, the more I plan to do
the less I get done as a general thing. But to-day was a
beautiful exception and my conscience is at peace. This
letter will be the coping stone to the fair edifice of a
good day's work.

. . .

Yes, I agree with you that all the trials of an uncongenial
environment should be regarded as *discipline*. I have
been led to this conclusion by the marked influence my
external surroundings and the life I have had to live for
the past eight years has had upon my own character. I
see now plainly that I *needed* the training very much and
that it has done me much good in many ways but chiefly
in enabling me to form habits of self-control. I used to
be a most impulsive, passionate creature. I do not use
the word passionate in the sense of bad temper for that
is not one of my besetting sins. But I used always to *rush
to extremes* in any emotion, whether of hatred, affection,
ambition or what not, that came uppermost. It was a
very serious defect and injurious to me in many ways,
mentally, morally, physically. I see now that it needed to
be corrected and the life I have had to live has been of
all others the one best calculated to correct it. I cannot
certainly say that it has been eradicated. I fear that,
given favorable circumstances, it might blaze up as

19

strongly as ever. But it certainly has been much modified and as a consequence I am a much more comfortable person both to others and to myself. In many other ways, too, my discipline has been of benefit. And, like you, I too hope that in time the training may be complete and I may be permitted to pass out into the fuller and broader life I long for. And I know one thing certainly. The discomfort and in many cases the absolute suffering I have undergone as a consequence of my environment has made me much more sympathetic for the failings and struggles and trials of others than I would otherwise have been—given me more insight into them—more understanding. It seems to me that the price I have paid has not been too great. I thought it was while I was paying it. But I know now that it was not.

Now for your difficulty—as far as I can grasp it. You find it hard to reconcile your literary ideal with your religious ideal. Now, I think that is because you have possibly too narrow a view of what religion really is—perhaps you are too much inclined to regard the *letter* as religion instead of the *spirit*. I do not think that you need feel worry because the line of work you take up may not be the highest. It may not be the highest absolutely but—for you—it is the highest relatively. The work God gives us to do and fits and qualifies us for doing must I think be *our* highest. I do not honestly think there is anything wrong in jokes or humor. Of course, there are *some* things too sacred and lofty to be profaned by jesting. But there are many others that are not. In these cases the jest is directed *not* against the things themselves but against travesties and mockeries of them, pretences of them where the spirit is absent although the letter is fulfilled. *I* think such humor is wholesome in its effect, purging away what might else bring the truths these shams stand for into contempt. Of course, I do not think *anyone* should ever pen a joke that is tainted with immorality, venom, vulgarity or sacrilege. But for all other kinds of humor I have only the heartiest appreciation and I think that the writer of it is doing quite as much for humanity as if he wielded a more serious pen. Often times a truth can be taught by a jest better than by earnest. I cannot think that everyone ought to write with only a "didactic or elevating purpose" in view. In fact, I question if *anyone* should or if any good is gained by so doing. I think we should just write out what is in us—what our own particular "demon" gives us—and the rest is on the knees of the gods. If we write truly out of our own heart and experience that truth will find and reach its own.

Yes, I *do* think that we are *always* "justified in proceeding along the line of least resistance"—that is I take it, in doing what comes easiest and best for us to do. To think otherwise would argue a purposelessness in God's dealings that I cannot admit—nay, a worse than purposelessness—positive cruelty in dealing with His creatures. Do not fear that it is "selfish to embark in a life that brings the greatest good to yourself alone." For the matter of that, any life that brings good to yourself must bring good first to other people—and that is enough, even if it be only the good of a laugh or a smile, a moment's relief from the cark and care of existence. I do *not* believe that God ever asks or wishes any man or woman "to forgo their ideals for the sake of another and more exacting path of service." *He* has fitted you for your ideal—He has given it to you; it is your duty, I firmly believe, to follow it up as best you may and develop it.

All I have to say is, if you feel that you are fitted for a literary life *go ahead* with it. I myself, never embarked on the literary life with any set purpose. But from childhood my one wish and ambition was to write. I never had any other or wished to have. When I grew up I began to write for the magazines tentatively while going to school and teaching school. Soon my success in it justified my putting all my effort and strength into it—I mean it was no longer necessary for me to do other work for a livelihood. My pen could support me and so I fairly became committed to a literary career. I am glad of it and I exult in my work. It is the greatest pleasure to me. But I *never* write of set purpose to do good or point a moral. When an idea comes to me I try to work it out as faithfully and artistically as possible and then send it out, confident that the pleasure I put into it will be reflected in the hearts of my readers. If I was honest in the work I did, good, honest, sincere work, even if only in the lesser paths, the lighter ways—do it, and your responsibility ends. This is my advice and I can add nothing more to it. But in the last analysis every soul must decide for itself—must stand or fall by its own light. I can only hope that whatever you decide will bring you the peace and strength of a problem solved.

.   .   .

I think it's an excellent idea—that of exchanging good quotations verses etc. with each other. I thought the poem you enclosed beautiful indeed. I enclose herewith a sonnet I found the other day and thought good and helpful. The other clipping is not intended for a literary gem but I merely send it as giving an account of a very interesting religious sect of which P. E. Island boasts a monopoly. They are known as McDonaldites after their founder[1] and are principally noted for "the works," a very strange manifestation of psychic excitement that comes over them in preaching. They will go through the wildest contortions, some of them impossible in a normal state, yet no injury ever results. They cannot resist the impulses of this strange power and the scenes at a McDonaldite sacrament are wild in the extreme. Out-

---

1. Rev. Donald McDonald (1783-1867), a member of the Church of Scotland (unattached), founded thirteen Mcdonaldite Churches which had some 5,000 adherents.

siders are often affected, even the most skeptical—and frequently take "the jerks" as bad as the sect themselves.

.   .   .

I am tearing over the paper at a perfectly reckless rate. I want to write a chapter in a serial story to-night yet. It is a very sensational yarn, written to suit the taste of the journal that ordered it and I don't care much for writing such but they give a good price for it. It deals with a lost ruby, a lunatic, an idiot boy, a mysterious turret chamber and a lot of old standard tricks like that. I've got to have it done by a certain date so I'm striving to finish it.

There are heaps of things I wanted to write about but 20 pages must be the limit to-night, or I shan't have any gray matter left for that blessed serial.

With all good wishes.

Yours sincerely,
L. M. Montgomery

Cavendish, P.E.I.
Can.

Sunday Afternoon
July 29, 1906

My dear Mr. McMillan:
It is a full fortnight since I took your letter out of my writing desk and put it in my portfolio to be answered at the first opportunity. And said opportunity never came till now. This is the season of the year when visitors abound and we have had company for the past three weeks, so that chances for letter writing were nil. Besides, the weather has been so warm and doggy that I have been going about in a half wilted condition and

when a spare moment or two would come I'd only feel like flinging myself down somewhere and doing and thinking absolutely nothing.

.　　.　　.

By the way our minister here is leaving us—Mr. McDonald[1]—and is going to Scotland for the winter. He will be attending college in Edinburgh I understand. I suppose it isn't in the least likely you'll ever run across him but of course it is possible. How far are you from Edinburgh? We are all very sorry that he is going away as he was well-liked and a successful pastor.

Bathing and swimming is the order of the day here now. Aunt May[2]—who is one of our visitors—and I go down for a "dip" nearly every evening and it is very jolly. I am persistently trying to learn to swim and now and then I flatter myself that I am really making progress but between whiles I have periods of deep discouragement. It seems to me a perplexing business.

This letter seems to me like something that is pasted together. I can't get any life into it. The day is so hot and I have a headache. So I will let it go for once and promise, like the naughty child, never to do so no more. I'm just as appreciative of your letter etc. as if I'd written twice as many pages with twice as much *reality* in them.

I remain as ever,

Yours most sincerely,

L. M. Montgomery

1. Rev. Ewen Macdonald (1870-1943), a Presbyterian minister, was born in Bellevue, Prince Edward Island. After completing his undergraduate studies at Prince of Wales College and Dalhousie University, he studied theology at Pine Hill Seminary in Halifax. In September, 1903, he came to Cavendish as minister of the Presbyterian congregation. He became secretly engaged to Maud Montgomery in 1906.

2. Mary Kennedy Macneill was married to L.M.'s uncle, the Rev. Leander Macneill.

Cavendish, P.E.I.
Can.

Sunday Evening
September 16, 1906

My dear Mr. McMillan:
It is high time I acknowledged that delightful "holiday"
epistle of yours which was incomparably the best of its
kind I ever received in my life. You would feel repaid
for the trouble you took in writing it if you knew how
much I enjoyed it; and of course the dainty "illustrations" added to its charm. I, alas, cannot return an epistle in kind for I've had no holiday or trip at all this summer. So I must do the best I can without.

.   .   .

So you partook of the delights of sea-bathing during
your jaunt. Isn't it delightful. I don't know anything I'd
rather do; and yet, do you know I very often have to
deny myself this pleasure because I *can't get anyone to go
bathing with me.* Here in this seaside village where almost
everybody has been born and bred in the salt air *nobody
but myself* ever goes bathing! Consequently I have to stay
home as I don't care to go alone, as the shore is about ¾
of a mile away, rather lonely and infested by lobster
fishermen. But I had a good summer this summer for
an aunt of mine was here for six weeks and we went almost every evening. Some of our dips were taken in a
heavy surf. It was the cream of bathing to stand there
and let a wave break up around one's neck in a glorious
smother of white foam. Sometimes they broke right
over our heads but I did not like *that* as it made one's
hair so wet and filled mouth and eyes with too much
brine. Our shore here seems remarkably like the one
shown in the views of your letter. I presume the rocks
on the Scottish shore are black or at least dark. Here

25

they are bright red, which gives a very vivid appearance in contrast to the blue sea and silvery white sand. As for my swimming I got on fairly well this summer but I shall never amount to much in this line. I am too big a coward and don't dare strike out into deep water.

.   .   .

To-day was Sunday and as we had no service in Cavendish I spent the greater part of the day alone in the woods. It was so beautiful there and really did me more good than church does *sometimes*. It was a mild dreamy September day and the woods were threaded all through with mellow golden sunshine and soft purry noises. They seemed to be resting—"we're done with growing and now we're just having a nice lazy, dreamful time" they seemed to say. Here and there amid all the green a scarlet leaf burned as if Autumn had walked through them and pushed a branch aside here and there leaving the stain of her fingers where they touched. The woods always seem to me to have a delicate, subtle life all their own that epitomizes the very spirit of all the seasons in turn and is never out of harmony with the time o' year. When I go to the shore I always like to have company—the greatness, the immensity, the illimitableness of the sea throws me back on myself and I yearn for human companionship. But in the woods I like to be alone for every tree is a true old friend and every tiptoeing wind a merry comrade. If I believe seriously in the doctrine of transmigration I should think I had been a *tree* in some previous stage of existence, I always feel so utterly and satisfyingly at home in the woods.

By the way, do you ever feel kindly inclined to that same doctrine of transmigration? It has a charm for me. In some moods I like to think of a succession of lives, following after each other with the restful sleep of death between, as the night between the busy waking days. It does not seem any more incredible than unending existence. Well, I'm getting into too deep waters, considering the lateness of the hour. Good-night and fair dreams of future holidays.

Very sincerely your friend,
L. M. Montgomery

Cavendish, P.E.I.
Can.

Monday Evening
April 1, 1907

My dear Mr. McMillan:

I don't know whether I can write a letter tonight but I mean to try. As a general rule I endeavor to write my letters only when I feel in the mood for it—and I'm afraid I don't feel so tonight. But just at present time is so precious with me that I can't waste any spare minutes and as I have a few tonight I mean to make the most of them answering your letter. For all the sins of omission I shall probably commit in it I ask your forgiveness beforehand. By the way, have you ever heard of the little boy who told his S. S. Superintendent that "sins of omission were sins we ought to have committed and didn't"? He was probably a connection of the little girl who said *faith* was "believing things you knew weren't true."

.　　.　　.

Yes, I agree with you that in marriage it is not desirable that likeness is found. In theory one would think it must be, but in reality it is very different. I believe that for *friendship* there should be similarity; but for love there must be dissimilarity. Of course, as I've never been mar-

27

ried my conclusions on the subject can hardly be considered final; but from *observation* I have decided that the happiest marriages I know are between people who are not at all alike, while some that are unhappy do exist between people who are very much alike. The trouble seems to be that two people finding themselves very harmonious in friendship jump to the conclusion that it will be just the same and even better in marriage. Their angles are similar and so when brought into the contact of an intimate union they jar on each other instead of fitting smoothly in.

Yes, it is very seldom indeed that a man and a woman can discuss *love* either pleasurably or profitably especially face to face. As you say, there is the danger of drifting into a flirtation or "platonics." Then again it is hard to separate self-consciousness from the subject. People are afraid to tell one what they really think about the matter—afraid that they will not be understood. I should be afraid myself in most instances. It is much easier to discuss it by letter. I can always *write* a great many things I could never *say*.

You ask:—

"Do you think that love depends upon an admiration for qualities possessed by the loved one? Or is it something more subtle than this?"

In answer to the first question I say most emphatically "NO." In explaining why I think so it will be necessary for me to inflict on you a bit of my own experience. Please regard it as quite impersonal, introduced merely to throw light on my conclusions.

I loved a man—let us call him A[1]—once. It was emphatically the love of my life. Yet mark this—I *did not respect him*—I did not *admire him in the least*. Before this experience I would have laughed at the idea that one *could* love a man they didn't respect. (The grammar of that

1. Herman Leard (1872-1899).

sentence is shocking but never mind!) Yet I certainly did. I would not have *married* him for anything. He was my inferior in every respect. This is not vanity on my part at all. He simply was. He had no brains, no particular good looks, in short, nothing that I admire in a man. Yet I loved him as I never can love any other man. There was about him "the subtle something" you speak of in the second part of your question. This man died and I have always been thankful that it ended so; because if he had lived I daresay I couldn't have helped marrying him and it would have been a most disastrous union in most respects. I feel sure this will all be rather unintelligible to you—it would have been to me before I underwent that experience.

Well, before I met A I had met a man whom I will call B.[2] He was *everything* that I admire in a man—he was handsome, brilliant, cultured, successful. *A* was not worthy to tie *B's* shoelace. Well, I liked *B* very much. I was very young and knowing nothing of love mistook my liking and admiration for love. I became engaged to him—and then simply *hated* him. Yes, laugh. I daresay you will. But it was no laughing matter to me—it was a tragedy. That man's kiss turned me cold with horror of it and of him—I *knew* I could *never* marry him. I tried for a year to be true to him and *hell* couldn't be worse than that year for me. In the end I told him the truth and broke the engagement. Immediately I was free. I *liked* him just as well as I had before that dreadful time, but I have been haunted ever since by the wretched conviction that I have spoiled his life. He has never married and says he can't forget.

Well, in those two experiences of mine you have all the answer I can make to your question. I loved one man in whom nobody could see anything to admire. I *couldn't* care for the other who was in all respects admi-

2. Edwin Simpson (1872-1949), from Belmont, Lot 16.

rable. If I had married B, I should have been unhappy all my life. If I had married *A* I should I believe have been *happy* but I would have deteriorated in every way—"lowered to his level," as Tennyson says. But Tennyson is not always right. When I was a schoolgirl I very much admired and believed a line in his poem "Lancelot and Guinevere."

"We needs must love the highest when we see it."

I don't believe it now. It is *not* true. We must *admire* the highest but *love* is an entirely different matter and is quite as likely to leave the best and go to the worst. Oh, it is a horribly perplexing subject and I grow dizzy thinking of it. I think, too, love varies very much with different temperaments. What would be true for me might be altogether false with a woman of a different temperament. But my own experience has taught me to understand a great many of the strange and perplexing happenings of life. The rules laid down in novels won't work out in real existence. I came across a bit of doggerel the other day that has more truth than poetry in it.

"There's a lot of things that never go by rule,
There's an awful lot of knowledge
That you never get at college,
There are heaps of things you never learn at school."
And that's about the way of it!

. . .

Now I've just got to finish this letter right up, owing to "circumstances over which I have no control." It isn't a satisfactory epistle, especially the part about *love* but I'll try to discuss that subject more lucidly in future. I've been interrupted a score of times since beginning.

Ever yours sincerely,
L. M. Montgomery

Cavendish, P. E. Island
Can.

Wednesday Evening
September 11th, 1907

My dear Mr. McMillan:

. . .

As we are discussing *love* I might as well take up that
part of your letter now. You ask "Is there any good to be
derived from living through an experience of unrequited love, compared with the veritable pain of such an
experience?"

My answer is emphatically "yes." To be sure, my love
was not "unrequited." But as it was for a man who was
my inferior and whom I could not for a moment think
of marrying, whom I knew I must put out of my life as
quickly and effectually as possible it was practically the
same thing, at least as far as the real pain was concerned, though of course I was spared the *humiliation.*
At the time I used to think *nothing* could ever compen-
sate for the suffering I endured or make it worth while;
but now when that pain has passed I see clearly how
vastly it enriched and deepened my life. I *wouldn't have
missed* that *experience* to be a saint in heaven!! *Nothing*
could atone to me for having missed it out of my life.
This is my exact feeling about it—that it would have
been the greatest misfortune that could have happened
to me not to have had it—that all the ages of eternity
could not make up for it.

You say "supposing an affinity does exist, is it possible
to fail to recognize that affinity when met face to face?"
Well, if you mean a first brief meeting I daresay it would
be very possible but if you mean somewhat continued
association I don't think there would be much danger.

31

But as I said in a former letter I don't believe three people in a thousand ever meet a perfect affinity. After all, this is a practical world and marriage must share in its practical ties. If two people have a mutual affection for each other, don't bore each other, and are reasonably well mated in point of age and social position, I think their prospects of happiness together would be excellent, even if some of the highest upflashings of the "flame divine" are missing. If I ever marry that is the basis on which I shall found my marriage. *But*—I shall never cease to thank fate that I *knew the other kind of love too.*   .   .   .

As to your question "What constitutes the attractive power between two people"—well, I'm afraid I'll only flounder here, too. Some say it is merely physical—the attraction of sex. I do not believe this because, as you say, it comes into question between members of the same sex. I have often met women to whom I have "taken" from the start; others—often excellent creatures—in whose company I am wretched beyond expression. Beauty, too, has little or nothing to do with it, even between the sexes. Some of the men who have thus attracted me have not been at all good-looking—although not of course actually *ugly*—while very handsome men have often repelled me markedly. I can't offer you any solution of this mystery. It is a most baffling one, dealing, it seems to me, with the very citadel of personality—the "Holy of Holies" in our souls.

I have a friend whom I love and in whose company I delight to be. She is the same with me. She has also another friend whom she loves and with whom she delights to be. This other friend is a good, refined, educated girl. I can't bear her. She bores me to misery. And she, on her part, can't understand what our mutual friend can see in me! There you are: What is the "whyness" in all this?

Speaking broadly I think that between woman and woman or man and man *likeness attracts;* between man and woman *unlikeness.*

As for people rarely marrying their first loves. Well, I have a rather practical explanation of that which may not please you but which I firmly believe to possess "more truth than poetry." Most men fall in love for the first time at so early an age that they simply can't *afford* to marry. They have to wait for a rise in salary or till they get through college etc. Before that time arrives they've got over the first attack—or the girl has married somebody else. I've heard it said, "Nine men out of ten never marry their first love. The tenth lives to repent it." I daresay it's true. Another saying is "A man always asks to be a woman's *first* love; a woman wishes to be a man's *last*." I can only speak from the woman's point of view of course; it is *true.* I should not care how many *predecessors* I had; but I *must have no successors.* What have you to say for the man's side.

I laughed over your remarks on the difficulty of getting well enough acquainted with a girl without raising gossip etc. But they're very true. It's the same everywhere I fancy. A girl can't be friends with a man but Mrs. Grundy begins to smirk and whisper. I don't know what is to be done, living in the kind of world we do. Perhaps "they manage these things better in Mars."

Then you proceed to ask a rather staggering question. "Is it true that the most important element in a girl's life is *love*."

Well, I suppose you must mean love for the opposite sex. Of course broadly speaking *love* is the most important element in *anyone's* life—man or woman,—love for home, parents, children, brothers, sisters, friends. I suppose what you mean is—is that all girls are thinking of in their relations to men friends? How can I tell? It never was in mine. Of course I expected to love and be loved some time. But I never remember thinking or wondering about any of my men friends "Is he going to love me etc. etc." Perhaps it was because I didn't want them to. They did very well as friends but would not have suited as lovers. I honestly believe a great many girls do really think a good deal about it. But I don't fancy this need make you overly "careful." A girl who would fall in love so easily or want a man to love her so easily would probably get over it just as quickly, very little the worse for wear. On the contrary, a girl who would take love seriously would probably be a good while finding herself in love and would require something beyond mere friendly attentions from a man before she would think of him in that light. Do you catch my meaning?

Moreover, I think men themselves are a good deal to blame. They say sometimes that they never pretended to anything but friendliness and it is not always true. I have heard several men say that and at the same time I knew positively that they had sometimes behaved in quite another fashion with the girls they were "going with"—attempting caresses, saying "sweet nothings" etc. They might not have "meant anything"—probably didn't; but a self-respecting and respected girl would have the right to think they did. Your sex is often as "flirtatious" as ours!!! As a rule, I believe that a man who treats a girl as he would wish another man to treat his sister need never be in any anxiety that she will misconstrue his friendliness before he has made up his mind about her. As for the gossip of "outsiders," nothing has ever been or ever will be discovered that will squelch that. The only thing is to totally disregard it. Before leaving the subject I may say I came across that poem on "Fate" and enclose it for you.

I've been busy all summer working on my new book—a "continuation" of my first. The latter isn't out yet. It is a juvenilish story of and for girls but I rather hope some grown-ups will like it, too. It is called "Anne of Green Gables" and the character of the little heroine is the motif of the book. My publishers want me to write a second one carrying her adventures further so I'm at it now. Book No. 1 is to be published on the usual ten per cent royalty basis. It will likely be out this fall. I shall send you a copy of course.

I have had some more things I wished to mention but it is so late I can't write more tonight so will close this letter.

My cat has just caught a *bat* and the commotion is terrible. I am torn between pity for the bat and horror of it. Bats are such uncanny things. I *can't* go and take it from puss; and yet the poor thing is squeaking so pitifully.

With all good wishes,

Yours most sincerely,
L. M. Montgomery

Cavendish, P. E. Island
Can.

Wednesday Evening
January 8, 1908

My dear Mr. McMillan:

.   .   .

Now for your letter:—

"When shall we be able to carry out our good resolutions?"

The "next day after never" dear friend. Be wise, like me, and give up making resolutions. It is a sign of extreme youth, which you ought to have left behind in your teens. Don't make any and then the wistful broken

35

ghosts of them will not lie in wait along your pathway, pouncing out on you just when you have made up your mind to be jolly and carefree. Time was when I made New Year Resolutions—a particularly ghastly species. I even wrote them down and tacked them up on the wall beside my looking glass, saying to myself, "Now, every time I break a resolution I'll mark a cross opposite it."

About the middle of February I would sneak down to the kitchen stove and poke those resolutions in, so covered with crosses that you'd have thought I'd been playing my childhood game of "Tit-tat-o" on the paper.

If, however, you want to make New Year Resolutions here are some differing from the common or grander kind in that they are not hard to keep.

1. I will not lose my temper but only mislay it occasionally.
2. I will never repeat gossip save to a trustworthy person.
3. I will try to improve other people's minds.
4. I will not get into anger if I can help it.
5. I will be kind and amiable when I feel like it.
6. I will try to bear other people's misfortunes with equanimity.
7. I will be cheerful when everything is going right.
8. I will go to church regularly on fine Sundays.
9. I will not tell anybody that he has a cold.
10. I will not growl at the weather when it is fine.

.　　.　　.

Do you take the "blues" too. I am selfishly *glad* to hear it. "Misery loves company" you know. I take them too—not very often but fearfully bad when I do have them. I cannot fully describe these experiences. They are not exactly mental—at least they are not produced by any outward circumstances, although of course they are aggravated by any worry or trouble. They *are dreadful,* far worse than physical pain. In so far as I can express my condition in words I feel a great and awful *weariness*—not of body or mind but of *feeling,* coupled with a strange dread of the future—*any* future, even a happy one—nay, a happy one most of all for in this strange mood it seems to me that to be happy would require more *emotional energy* than I will possess. At such times the only future to which I could look forward with resignation would be a colorless existence making absolutely no demands on my emotional nature. I am bankrupt in hope and self-confidence. Another curious thing about these moods is that while I am in them I am thoroughly convinced that I shall always feel like that. It is no use to tell myself that I have felt so before and got over it. "Yes, *those* moods passed away but *this* will be permanent," is the unreasonable answer my suffering consciousness makes. This condition lasts three or four days, then vanishes as suddenly as it came. I am quite likely to re-act to the opposite extreme—to feel rapturously that the world is beautiful and mere existence something to thank God for.

I suppose our "blues" are the price we have to pay for our temperament. "The gods don't allow us to be in their debt." They give us sensitiveness to beauty in all its forms but the shadow of the gift goes with it.

. . .

I saw Mr. McDonald on his return from Scotland and he told me of writing you. Your good opinion seems to have been mutual. He is at present settled in the Bloomfield congregation, about sixty miles from here.

My *book* is to be out soon. I had a letter from my publishers the other day. At present we are wrangling over the author's name. I want it published under the name "L. M. Montgomery" as all my work has been. The Page Co. insist on "Lucy Maud Montgomery" which I loathe.

Don't know who will come out on top—probably the publishers. You shall have a copy as soon as the book comes out.

.   .   .

This is quite an extent of space to say good-night in but I must close like the immortal Sam Weller with "a rayther sudden pull-up," as I'm wanted elsewhere.

Bon Voyage to you through '08.

Very sincerely yours,
L. M. Montgomery

Cavendish, P. E. Island
Can.

Monday Afternoon
Aug. 31, 1908

My dear Mr. McMillan:
After vainly trying for several weeks to get time to answer your letter "at one fell swoop" I have decided that it must be done, if it is ever to be done at all, on the instalment plan. I'll write a page or two every spare ten minutes I have and if the result is "patchy" blame the government, who *will* have only 24 hours in a day.

I have one "big" letter of yours to answer and two notes, so will take them as they come. Oh, I've had such a busy summer!!!!

I am glad you liked my book,—at least, as far as you had read. No, *nothing* in the tone of your former letters made me "suspect flattery." I simply warned you not to say you liked it if you didn't because I feared that, when you had been given a copy of the book you might not like to criticize it frankly and might let your politeness get the better of your discernment.

As you say, the "get up" of the book is excellent. I am

well pleased with my publishers. It seems to be selling very well also. Though only published June 10th the fourth edition went to press to-day and is almost all ordered ahead. The publishers are certainly advertising it well. I think I sent you a copy of a poster they got out for it.

But talk of reviews! I subscribed to a clipping bureau and they come in shoals every day. So far I have received sixty-six of which sixty were kind and flattering beyond my highest expectations; of the remaining six two were a mixture of praise and blame, two were contemptuous and two positively harsh. However, the nice ones are so much in the majority that these adverse ones do not worry me much. One criticism was correct—it said the ending of the book was too "poor and commonplace" to match the "freshness and originality" of the first two thirds. One denounced my heroine as "impossible, mawkish and tiresome." She might be two out of the three but how could the "impossible" be "tiresome." Whatever else it might be I don't think it would be that. Another said "she combined the sentimentality of an Alfred Austin with the vocabulary of a Bernard Shaw." On the other hand the favorable critics call her "charming" "vivid" "original," "one of the most delightful characters in juvenile fiction" etc. etc. One thing surprises me in the reviews and one thing disappoints me. I am surprised that they seem to take the book so seriously— as if it were meant for grown-up readers and not merely for girls. The disappointment comes in this:—I had hoped to *learn* something from the reviews. I knew the book must have faults which its author could not perceive and I expected the reviews would point them out. But there is no agreement. What one critic praises as the most attractive feature in the book another condemns as its greatest fault—and there am I no wiser than before.

•　　•　　•

Tuesday Morning

I have just come in from my usual morning walk over the hill—which I always take after I've done my morning "chores," before sitting down to write. It's a pearl of a day and the old hill road is lovely. Just now it is scarfed with a ribbon of golden rod and airy smoke blue asters—so beautiful and yet suggestive of sadness in that they are the forerunners of autumn. In fact the country people hereabouts call asters by the pretty poetic name of "farewell summers." Last night was very like the fall—cold and windy with a red sunset sky and a pale new moon. But today is warm and purple-hazy again—summer is still with us but her glances are backward now. Well, I like autumn too. Indeed I think every season has dear lovable charms of its own, and I'm sure I'd get frightfully tired of everlasting summer. A Canadian winter has a wonderful zest and sparkle and even the storms have a wild white majesty of their own. A still winter evening among the wooded hills with the sunset kindling great fires in the westering valleys is something I would not exchange for a month of hot July days.

I have received a great many letters since the publication of my book, from editors and readers. They are so kind and appreciative that they encourage me vastly. But of course there is a seamy side to it too. I am pestered with letters from tourists who are holidaying on the Island who say they have read my book and want to "meet" me. I dislike this kind of publicity and avoid it whenever possible. I don't want to be "met." I finished my second "Anne" book the other day and am now revising it and later on will have to typewrite it. I began it last winter at the request of the publishers, supposing I'd have plenty of time to do it in. But since the first one has caught on they have been urging me to have it ready by October. As a result I have been writing furiously all through this hot summer. For this reason I don't think the book is as good—comparatively speaking—as the first. But I may not be able to judge—I feel so soaked and saturated with "Anne" that I'm sick of the sound of her name. The fact is, I've rather overworked of late and am feeling far from well. I don't seem to have any nervous energy—I'm deadly tired all the time, feel as if I wanted in Kipling's words "to lie down for an aeon or two" before I'd get thoroughly rested. When I get my book off I am going to take a rest. I'd like to go off somewhere for a little trip but of course, I can't do that as I can't leave grandma. My "nerves" have been in a bad condition ever since a shock I had three weeks ago. The kitchen roof caught fire on a windy day. I knew that by the time any outside help came it would be too late, so I dragged a ladder from the barn, got it up somehow, mounted it with a pail of water and succeeded in putting out the fire. Then I simply collapsed and couldn't lift my head for the rest of the day. Have been feeling the bad effects ever since.

This letter is not the sort of letter—in quality at least—which I would wish to send. I have written it at a dozen odd moments and have felt too tired and "driven" to do justice to myself or my correspondent. When the cool winter days and long quiet evenings come I'll promise better things. Meanwhile, "to understand is to forgive" and I'm sure you'll do both.

Very sincerely yours,
L. M. Montgomery

Cavendish, P.E.I.
Can.

Friday Evening
May 21, 1909

My dear Mr. McMillan:
I have been waiting to answer your letter until I could
be sure of an uninterrupted space of time—for I dislike
to write a letter, such as our correspondence requires,
by fits and starts. But I fear it will have to be written so,
or not at all; so I shall begin it tonight. When I can finish
it I cannot predict. It may be the product of a dozen different moods ere it is finished. Just now, at least, I am in
a *good* mood. We have had a delicious day of sunshine
and growth which, coming after a dreary week of northeast wind and drizzle, when the very world seemed
weeping over its inability to advance one step spring-
ward, has been a mental and spiritual tonic. (The subject and verb in the foregoing sentence are nearly as far
apart as a German could put them.) This is a rare evening of pale greennesses and wild wettish perfumes;
and the thought of what the woods back over the hill
must be just now is at once a boon and a torture. I would
go to them if it were possible; but I have an engagement
this evening and could not get back in time for it.

I received your card from Perth lately and one some
time ago announcing your success with the daffodil
bulb. Am glad it turned out so well. Just leave it where it
is; it need never be moved but will "increase and multi-
ply." Be particular never to cut the foliage until it yel-
lows down of its own accord. If you do the size of next
year's blossoms—if indeed it should bloom at all—will
be sadly decreased. For this reason daffodils should
never be planted where a lawn mower is to pass—which
is a pity, since they are especially charming amid grass.
They are as hardy as weeds and *need* no winter protec-

42

tion; but I think when it is given the flowers are larger. Dead leaves and boughs will do: but better still is a mulch of well-rotted cow manure if you can obtain it. Bulbs like rich feeding, although they will do very well without it.

I was very glad to hear that you are feeling better. So am I: we are to be congratulated accordingly for health is a most priceless treasure and we cannot hope to accomplish much without it. I was not at all well all winter. My nerves were in a bad state. But I feel so much better now. I did not write much all winter and the rest did me good. Speaking of writing—I sent you a serial of mine a little while ago—"Una of The Garden." Hope you received it all right and that it did not share the fate of the *Anne* poster—of which I haven't another copy to send. I sent it in a stout mailing tube and it should not have gone astray.

No, I didn't have the least trouble opening the box of creepers. The cover came off easily. Probably some curious post-office or Customs official had been at it before me. I planted the creepers as soon as it was possible but they haven't come up yet—no wonder, for our spring has been horribly cold and wet. I hope they will grow for the sake of the ocean they crossed.

Thank you for the review of Anne you sent. I had not otherwise seen it, though my clipping bureau sent me a good many of the English reviews. The *Spectator* review tickled me not a little—it was so kind and occupied nearly two columns. Had anyone told me that the revered Spectator would treat my book as of any importance at all I would have laughed the idea to scorn. But it did. I don't know whether Pitmans advertise very much but as Anne is in her fifth English edition, she isn't doing so badly. She is in her eleventh edition in America. I am now correcting the proofs of the new *Anne* book which is not to be out till the fall. The reason for this postponement is quite an agreeable one. Pages write me that the sales of *Anne* have not yet shown any signs of falling off and they don't want to give her a rival as long as this continues. They are urging me to work at a new book but I haven't the "grit" for it yet. I've an idea in my head for one, however, but it must grow a good while yet. Besides as we used to say at school, I don't see any good "killing myself to keep myself alive."

You speak of my having *three* styles. I daresay that is true. But the style of *Anne* is my *real* style. The others are only skilfully assumed garments to suit the particular story being "built." I wrote *Anne* in my *own* style, and I think that is the secret of her success.

Thank you for the "bookshelf" you sent me. But that "interview" was a "fake"—built, I suppose, out of scraps of information furnished by my publishers. The personal paragraph must have been the product of somebody's "imagination" helped out a little by my photo. It jarred on me horribly. I don't care what they say about my book—*it* is public property—but I wish they would leave my ego alone. However, I suppose notoriety is the unpleasant shadow always cast by even a little fame.

.   .   .

Tuesday Evening, May 25

Here beginneth the second lesson! Not a "speck" of time have I had since I was last interrupted until now.

My hieroglyphics are a little worse than usual. I have just come in from an errand and have carried a clumsy parcel in my right hand for over a mile. As a result I can hardly hold the pen and my fingers are badly cramped.

My errand took me to the shore tonight. The shore was, as is usual now, rather quiet and lonely. When I was a child it was not so. Those were the days of the mackerel fishing and the shore was dotted with fishing houses. I used to spend much time at the shore, being often sent there on errands, such as to get a fish or gather dulse. I knew every cove and headland and rock on the shore, and all the stories and legends connected with them. The tale of the terrible "Yankee Storm" or American Gale was one of great interest. This was a fearful storm in 1851, where hundreds of American fishing vessels were wrecked on the north shore. One of the most striking and pathetic tales connected with this storm was that of the *Franklin Dexter,* a vessel which went ashore on Cavendish rocks. All on board were lost, including four brothers, the only sons of their father, who lived in Massachusetts. After the storm their bodies came ashore and were buried in the graveyard. Their father, a broken hearted old man, came on to C. and insisted on having the bodies exhumed, saying that their mother had bid him bring her boys home to her. The coffins were put on board a sailing vessel at the harbor, where the father himself returned home in a passenger vessel. The sailing vessel left the harbor with the four bodies on board *and was never heard of again.* It seemed as if it were a thing fore-ordained that those bodies should never rest under turf. I have also heard my grandfather[1] say that the captain of the vessel was determined to sail out of the harbor on a night when the tide rendered it difficult to get out. He was told that he wouldn't get out that night and he retorted with an oath that he would sail out of the harbor that night if he sailed straight to hell! He *did* sail out of the harbor—and, as aforesaid, neither the ship nor any on board of her, was ever heard of more.

•   •   •

Away to the westward, across the harbor, the view was bounded by New London Cape, a long sharp point run-

1. Alexander Marquis Macneill (1820-1898).

45

ning far out to sea. In my childhood I never wearied of speculating on what might be beyond that point—a very realm of enchantment I felt sure. Even when I gradually grew into the understanding that beyond it was merely another reach of shore just like our own it still held a mystery and a fascination for me. I longed to stand out on that remote purple peak, beyond which was the land of lost sunsets. Of late years a new charm has been added to it—a revolving light which, seen from here, flashes on the point in the dusk of summer nights like a beacon "on the foam of perilous seas in fairylands forlorn."

As I came home in the afterlight I saw a sight that filled me with rapture. To my right was a cluster of tall, gently waving spruces. Seen in daylight, those spruces are old and uncomely—dead almost to the tops, with withered branches. But seen in that enchanted light, against a sky that began by being rosy saffron, and continued to be silver green, and ended finally in crystal blue, they were like dark, slender witch-maidens weaving their spells of magic in a rune of elder days. How I longed to share in their gramarye—to have fellowship in their twilight sorceries.

I have been lately reading Keats for the first time. I do not think I like him. He is full of beauty—but it seems to me too sensuous and lavish a beauty. I like a beauty with some austerity and restraint. Nevertheless, here and there occur lines that are exquisite. For example,

"He ne'er is crowned
With immortality who fears to follow
Where airy voices lead."

If he had never written anything but that he would have been a poet.

Since the publication of *Anne* I have received many requests for stories from editors of "big" magazines, many of whom have been turning down my work for several moons. They seem willing to take anything now.

. . .

Did you receive the copy of the "Island Hymn"[2] I sent you at New Year's?

Well, sixteen double pages mean thirty-two of my ordinary ones, and as it is getting late and I am very tired after a busy day I'll say good-night for this time.

Very faithfully yours,
L. M. Montgomery

Cavendish, P. E. Island

Sunday
Feb. 20, 1910

My dear Mr. McMillan:
I had no idea it was going to be this long before I should get around to answering your letter. It was not for lack of time—I had too much time. But ever since New Year's I have been suffering from a nervous breakdown and my doctor advised me to do as little mental work, even letter writing, as possible. I suffered from insomnia and a dreadful sort of *restlessness,* which when it took possession of me seemed to unfit me utterly for doing anything which required the least thought. I am better now, however, and feel that it is a pleasure, rather than an effort to write letters, so I am getting one a day written and this morning yours is on the top of the pile.

I overworked myself before Christmas. You will remember that last spring I sent you my serial story "Una of The Garden." Well, my publishers thought that if this

---

2. L. M. composed this hymn in 1908, and it has become the Island anthem.

story were a little longer it would do very well to be issued in book form. Accordingly about the middle of
November I went to work at it. I had to have it done by
the first of the year. It was originally about 24,000
words long. I expanded it to 48,000. This meant writing
it over twice and as the time was short I had to crowd
three months work into six weeks. I had besides to suffer a good deal of worry connected with family and personal concerns; and altogether, as I have said, the result
was a nervous breakdown. The suffering of nervous
maladies is quite indescribable. I should far rather endure physical pain. Apart from the restlessness which
was so marked a feature of my case, the most distressing
symptom seemed to be a horrible *dread* of the future—of
any future. I felt frightened of life—*any* life, even a most
happy and pleasant one. If you have never experienced
this feeling you cannot realize how hideous it is—and
how unconquerable, since its seat seems to be in the sub-
conscious mind, and cannot be reached or cured by reason or any effort of will.

But I am thankful to say that I am much better now
and I am very thankful.

.   .   .

In regard to *Una of The Garden,* it will be published in
book form under another title, "Kilmeny of the Orchard." The heroine's name is changed, at my publishers' request, and I changed the scene from a garden to
an orchard, because I thought the garden resembled
too closely the description of Hester Gray's garden in
Avonlea. The book is to be illustrated in color by Gibbs. I
expect the critics will think I rush from one extreme to
the other. In my first book I had a heroine who talked
all the time. In my third book I have one who cannot
talk at all. Charlotte Brönte tried the experiment of
making a *plain* heroine; there have been *blind* heroines;

but as far as my memory goes, I don't think anyone ever ventured on a dumb heroine before. I think the "padding" necessary to increase the length weakened the story very much and it was against my better judgment that I consented to have it appear in book form at all. It will probably sell quite well, on the strength of my other books, but I feel the purchasers will consider themselves "sold." Besides, it is of a very different style from the *Anne* books and that is always a dangerous experiment with a public who have learned to expect a certain style from an author.

In regard to *plots*—well, I always keep my notebook handy and jot down any idea for plot, character, or incident which occurs to me. Then I take a plot which appeals to me and select characters and incidents to harmonize. The whole plot of Una—or Kilmeny as we must call her now—grew out of this motif suggested by an old tale I had read somewhere of a boy at the court of Alexander the Great who couldn't speak until one day he saw his father in a position of great danger. "Boy *cannot* speak because his mother would not." When I came to write the story I saw how much more suggestive it would be to have the central figure a girl and all the rest grew naturally out of this germ. Curiously enough, after the publication of the serial I had a letter from a woman who told me that her little girl of ten was just like "Una" and the doctors explained it the same way. She wrote very appealingly to know if my story had any foundation in fact, as if it had she would have some hope that her daughter might speak some day. The doctors, she said, thought the child might learn gradually to speak. The child's dumbness it seems, resulted, not from any stubborn refusal on the mother's part to speak, but as a result of a terrible pre-natal shock of fright, which robbed the mother of the power to speak for several weeks. It was all very interesting—and pitiful, as I could not give her any facts of action regarding the reality of

49

my plot. I was much interested in the anecdote you wrote about the paralytic lady and her sailor son. I believe these things do happen, subject to laws about which we as yet know little or nothing.

.   .   .

"Anne of Green Gables" sold better this year than last, which my publishers tell me is a very uncommon thing. I suppose the two books help to sell each other. I have been flooded with letters entreating me to write a third Anne book and the Page Co. are also very anxious for it; but I feel as if I simply could not do it. The freshness has gone out of the *Anne* idea. It may return some day. But unless it does I shall never throw any further light on Anne's career. That must be left to the "scope of the imagination."

.   .   .

Swedish and Dutch editions of Green Gables have appeared. "Anne of Gron Kulla" is the Swedish equivalent of the title. I had a very charming letter from its translator, Mrs. Karin Jensen of Stockholm. She also sent me a Swedish review but of course I couldn't read a word of it. She said it was a very nice one however.

This is a very poor sort of letter but as you understand, I am not yet well enough to write anything in the way of a literary production so please overlook all defects. I shall hope to be able to do better next time. Your last letter was most interesting, especially in your account of the *ghost.*

With all good wishes.

Sincerely yours,
L. M. Montgomery

Cavendish, P. E. Island
Can.

Thursday
Sept. 1, 1910

Dear Mr. McMillan:

. . .

It is a beautiful September morning, with just a hint of
the night's frost in the air still. By and by the sun will
mellow it out; but in the evening it will creep back again.
"The turn of the season" has come; and though we may
have many delicious weeks yet, they are the weeks of
autumn, not of summer. I am taking today as a sort of
holiday. I shall write your letter this morning and the afternoon I shall spend in the woods, dreaming. This is by
way of celebrating the conclusion of my new book "The
Story Girl" which I finished yesterday. I think it is a
good piece of work. It gave me great pleasure to write it,
so it ought to give people pleasure to read it. From a literary point of view I think it is the best thing I've done
yet, but I question if it will be as popular as "Anne" for
all that. It may possibly run as a serial in some magazine
this winter. It will not be out in book form until next
spring. I have been working very hard at it all summer.
Now I am going to take a two months vacation from literary work, and have a good idle autumn. I cannot get
away for a trip but I shall have a good time at home, taking long rambles, reading lots of new books—and old
ones—and *just lounging*.

An Uncle and his family from St. John, N.B. spent
July and August with us, as usual. He is a nervous in-
valid and his entertainment is a somewhat difficult matter. I felt the strain of it a good deal. . . . I am not as well
as I might be, though vastly better than I was last winter.

The truth is I am rarely free from worry of one kind or another, owing mainly to grandmother's great age and consequent inability to see anything from any point of view but her own. I am stating this merely as a fact, not a complaint, that you may understand why my existence is generally one of continued worry. When we have company all the unpleasant conditions are aggravated. Hence my summer has not been an agreeable one, and I look forward to a quiet and peaceful autumn as a "consummation devoutly to be wished."

.   .   .

Thanks muchly for your most kind reviews of the *Annes* and *Kilmeny*. The proportion of favorable and unfavorable reviews of the latter have been about the same as in the Anne case. The English reviews have all been kind with one exception, and much more *discriminating* than the American reviews. The latter seemed to regard the book merely as agreeable summer fiction. The former took notice of the psychological interest and the development of the plot. The exception aforesaid, was the *Clarion*, which wrote a review so venomous that, had it been in a Canadian or American journal I should have thought personal spite was at the root of it. Here it is:—

Clarion Review

"Kilmeny of the Orchard is a terrible specimen of the American novel of sentiment. It is a product of the same industrious pen which created 'Anne of Green Gables,' and it is a similar book, only more so. Anne merely caused one to feel faint; Kilmeny brings on a bilious headache. She is a poor dumb girl of extraordinary beauty and stupidity, who stands about in a Canadian orchard while the hero waits 'for the undisguised light of welcome that always leapt into her eyes at the sound of his footsteps.' He (the hero) is a Canadian 'college boy' who goes to play at schoolmastering in the vicinity of Kilmeny's orchard. His name is Eric and after calm and judicious consideration, he declares his love for the dumb girl, which that young person rejects in Eric's own interest, for she believes (mistakenly as we think) that it is necessarily bad for a man to be married to a dumb wife. Eric accordingly grows thin and miserable, but one day when he is brooding in the orchard (Kilmeny's orchard) a hated rival appears in the person of an Italian youth, bearing the singular name of Neil Gordon. Mr. Gordon, taking Eric unawares rushes at him with a hatchet but the dumb girl, appearing at this critical moment, finds her voice and cries out 'Eric, Eric, look behind you.' The rival slinks away and the dumb girl 'sunned over with smiles' flung herself on Eric's breast. Also she utters the following words, 'Oh Eric, I can speak—I can speak. Oh, it is so wonderful! Eric, I love you—I love you.' We observe that the 'Spectator' in reviewing 'Anne of Green Gables,' stated that the book was 'in direct lineal descent from the works of Miss Alcott.' Our own childish recollections of the works of Miss Alcott are kindly but dim. We shall not attempt, therefore, to probe the ancestry of Miss Montgomery's newest book. It is enough for us to know that it tells a childish and improbable story in commonplace language and a gushing manner."

Ha-hem! How's that for high? The Clarion reviewed the Anne books favorably, so it must have a new reviewer. I'm obliged to him for a good laugh. Some of the unfavorable reviews, being couched in temperate language and remarking upon real faults, I took seriously. But the *Clarion's* merely amused me. For contrast here is the *London World* review.

"The delicacy and charm of the love idyll which Miss Montgomery gives her readers in this, her latest book, are so subtle that it is almost impossible to suggest the story in a few words without spoiling it. The whole is so slight, yet admirably balanced, the background of tragedy and pain is touched in with so true a restraint, the art which pervades every page is so refined, that the cultivated imagination will return to the story again and again in memory to find always something fresh to enjoy. Miss Montgomery is a poet and an idealist, rather than a student of character. Kilmeny is a dream rather than a girl, and it would be hard to find a prototype for her lover among the young men of today. But it would be no less hard to find in the field of fiction today word-painting to equal the first description of Kilmeny as she makes music in the orchard, or that tragic bit of description, later in the story, which tells why Kilmeny has not the gift of speech. Nine novels out of ten seem to have been written in a hurry in order to be read, in a hurry and thrown aside. But to appreciate work like this we must find or make an hour's leisure and bring our taste and judgment to bear upon what has been created with thought and care for their delectation."

· · ·

Your comment on the last illustration in Kilmeny is perfectly correct. Artists are always making those mistakes. They don't study the letter press half carefully enough. I do not really think there ought to be illustrations in a novel at all—unless the author could draw them. If anyone else draws them his conception of the characters is never the same as the author's. Gibbs' Kilmeny is beautiful but she is not *my* Kilmeny. I picture her as *whiter*,—a rose-white face with dark blue eyes and black hair. Gibbs gives her a ripe, ruddy look which I do not like. By the way, can you tell me the proper pronunciation of "Kilmeny." Is is "Kil-menny"—or "Kilmeeny." Nobody on this side of the Atlantic seems to know, and she gets both. When people ask me, "How is the name of your heroine pronounced?" I have to admit that I don't know myself. And then they *look* at me!

.   .   .

Good-bye for this time. With all good wishes, I am
                                    Yours sincerely,
                                    L. M. Montgomery

Park Corner, P. E. Island

Thursday
May 4, 1911

My dear Mr. McMillan:
Your letter of February 28th reached me during the most sorrowful period of my life. I am long in answering it, but you will understand why when I tell you that on March 5th my dear old grandmother, who has been the only mother I ever knew, became ill with pneumonia and five days later passed peacefully away. She was almost eighty-seven years old and I knew I could not hope to have her with me very much longer. But that did not make the parting any easier when it came.

Then family reasons necessitated the immediate breaking up and departure from my old home and haunts. This was—and is—such an anguish to me that I cannot write of it. I came over to Park Corner, where I am at present staying with an aunt.[1] It is a beautiful spot

---

1. Annie (Macneill) Campbell (1848-1924), the wife of John Campbell (1833-1917), was the eldest sister of L.M.'s mother, Clara Woolner Montgomery (1853-1876).

here—a big farmhouse surrounded by orchards and beech woods with a splendid pond before the door. I have often spent pleasant visits here and love it—but it isn't home. And I do get so horribly lonely and homesick at times especially at night. When these long beautiful spring evenings come it seems to me that I shall *die* if I cannot go to Lover's Lane and wander through it, going home by starlight over the hill, to see the old home light gleaming from the trees as it gleamed for over eighty years. It hurts me so to think of the old house left desolate and forsaken, with no life in its rooms, no fire glowing on its hearth. Yet I am thankful that dear grandma did not suffer and that she died in her own home surrounded by beloved and familiar faces. For her, at least, all is well. And as her later years were embittered by the ingratitude and neglect of a son[2] who owed her more than most sons do, I cannot but feel thankful that her heart can never more be pierced by his unfilial conduct. But for those of us who are left behind there is the bitterness of the breaking of a lifelong tie.

Well, I shall say no more about this. It hurts me too much. Instead I shall take up your letter and try to answer it as of old.

.   .   .

I have been reading the proofs of my new book ever since coming over, and finished recently. It will soon be out. I do not know the exact date. I feel strangely little interest in it. I do not even seem to care whether it succeeds or falls flat. Eyes are closed forever that would have loved to read it.

I never have any difficulty getting the consent of the

2. John Franklin Macneill (1851-1936).

magazines for the republication of any articles. It is an understood thing on this side of the water that a magazine holds only the rights of serial publication. However, now that I have become something of a celebrity I make assurance doubly sure by reserving all rights except serial rights when I offer the article.

.   .   .

And now about my summer and future plans. I have something to tell you which may surprise you a little. Early in July I expect to be married to the Rev. Mr. Macdonald[3] whom you met in Scotland. He is now settled in Leaskdale, Ontario. We have been engaged for five years but as I could not leave grandmother as long as she wished to remain in her old home our engagement was kept secret. We have decided now that it would be foolish to wait any longer. So we shall be married early in the summer and we are going over to spend three months or at least two and a half "doing" England and Scotland. At least, that is our plan at present, if nothing occurs to prevent it. I have had so many plans set aside lately that I cannot convince myself that anything else will come to pass as expected. If we go over it will be the realization of a long cherished dream. I feel sure I shall enjoy it, but at present everything seems so shadowed by the sorrow of the past winter that I cannot feel the pleasure in it I would have felt had it been possible to go while grandmother was still alive.

Of course we must arrange a meeting. If you would

---

3. She now spells his name correctly, having before spelled it McDonald. Later she will spell his first name Ewan rather than Ewen. Note also that she spells George Boyd's surname incorrectly until later in 1911, when she finally writes it MacMillan. Later, she spells her best friend's name Frederica rather than Fredericka.

like us to visit Alloa we shall be delighted to go. If it would suit you better to meet us elsewhere that will be all right, too. Couldn't you arrange to spend your vacation "doing" some special country with us? I want to see the Scott country, especially the *Marmion* and *Lady of the Lake* district. I want to go to "Kirriemuir" and see the scenes of Barries novels—in short I want to see every notable place, I've read about. I don't know where we shall land but probably in Liverpool. We shall likely sail on the first suitable steamer leaving Montreal after July 1st. I shall write you definitely about this later on, and when we reach there. I think my "working" address will likely be the Canadian office, 17 Victoria Street London. Or will you let me have my letters addressed to "34 Castle St. Alloa" and forward them to me, if it won't be too much trouble—at least while we are in Scotland. We can make all definite arrangements later.

It will seem strange to meet in person, will it not, after our long impersonal friendship. I wonder if we shall be able to be as frank and open with each other as our letters have been. Or will some unknown elusive barrier of personality rear itself between us to the undoing of all good comradeship? I sincerely hope not, but it is impossible to foretell. We cannot control such things by wish or will. No matter how smoothly the machinery of mental affinities runs, some little jog of temperament may throw the whole thing out of focus. (The confusion of metaphors in that sentence is fearful.)

But let us hope not, I do not think it will be so. I fancy we'll be as good chums face to face as on paper.

I have recently got a dandy new camera. It is a kodak. My old camera did excellent work but it was very slow. It was no good for snapshots and I could not use film cartridges in it. My new one is said to be the best made. I intend to take it abroad with me, well provided with cartridge films, and shall hope to get many souvenirs of my trip.

I can't really believe I am going, though. I am sure something will turn up to prevent it!

I must close now. My address will be as below till the last of June.

Yours sincerely,
L. M. Montgomery

Park Corner
P. E. Island
Can.

Park Corner, P.E.I.

June 5, 1911

Dear Mr. MacMillan:

This is just a hurried note in answer to your letter. I am *so* busy that I haven't time to turn round!

I am to be married on July 5 and on July 8th we sail from Quebec on the *Megantic* for Liverpool. Arriving there we shall likely go to Glasgow for the Exhibition. This will give us time to communicate with you and adapt our plans to yours. I think your idea of spending a week at Spittal an excellent one. Select whatever time suits yourself. Please, as you suggest, secure accommodation for us at your boarding house there and make all necessary arrangements. Anytime after we get there will suit us. We shall "do" Scotland first and then England.

I quite understand your position in regard to our going to Alloa. Do not fear that I shall feel offended in any way. I wanted to see Alloa, because it was your home, and if we can spend a day there we shall just go to a hotel. All these are minor things. The main point is to meet personally and have a pleasant time together.

This is, as I have said, a mere note. I shall have time for no more letters till next fall. I sent you a copy of The

Story Girl. If anything further occurs to me shall drop you a line.

Yours in hope of a merry meeting ere long,

L. M. Montgomery

On board S.S. "Megantic"

July 15, 1911
Saturday

Dear Mr. MacMillan:
We are nearing Liverpool after a most delightful voyage. We have had ideal weather and no trace of sea-sickness. If possible we shall go on to Glasgow tonight. If not, as soon as we can. We shall go to St. Enoch's Hotel at Glasgow and shall be there or leave our address there while we stay. We shall take in the Exhibition so will be there for Monday and Tuesday anyhow I expect, and perhaps longer if we decide to take any excursions from there. I telegraphed you today so shall hope to hear from you regarding your plans as soon as convenient. This note is merely to explain wire more fully.

Yours sincerely,

L. M. Montgomery Macdonald

Russell Hotel
London
Sept 19, 1911

My dear Mr. MacMillan:
Your letter of the 18th came to hand this morning. I have just a few minutes to write a hurried answer. We had intended going to Ireland this morning, do-ing Dublin and Killarney and joining our boat at

60

Queenstown. But the railway strike in Ireland has skied all that. So we shall remain quietly here until Thursday, then go to Liverpool to join our boat. We shall make good use of our time seeing some spots in London we thought we should have to cut out.

Any mail which comes after this send to "The Manse, Leaskdale, Ontario."

We had a pleasant luncheon with the business manager of the Pitman Pub. Co. last week; and a lady journalist and ardent suffragette called to interview me one evening. That is all—and quite enough, if all the journalists here could question as she did! I was interested in hearing of the ministerial reference to "Anne."

I hope your Exhibition Essay will capture everything in sight.

I wonder if there is anything in that cow and snake story. It is very curious.

Saturday we went down to Dunwich in Suffolk, where grandmother was born and lived until she was twelve. It is a very quaint, slow, out of the world place right by the sea. We found the old Woolner homestead without much trouble. It is a beautiful old place and as the house is at present unoccupied we got the key and went all over it. You can imagine my emotion. I was told it was all unchanged since the Woolner's day. The house is of brick and the floors of stone. Great grandmother Woolner's garden, hawthorn enclosed, is still there. If only poor grandma were alive to hear about it! But her sister, Aunt Margaret, aged 89, is still alive and remembers her old home well, as she was 14 when she left it. I must write her and send her a picture of it. I took several.

The day we went to Windsor Castle we saw a flying machine. I can't tell you how I felt when I saw it, soaring as gracefully as a great bird athwart the sunset sky. I actually trembled with emotion.

That same evening we went to see "MacBeth," with

61

Beerbohm Tree in the name part. It was good. But I thought they "played to the gallery" a good deal, especially in regard to the supernatural effects. I suppose they have to to "make Shakespeare pay."

I shall write you when I get home and settled. We are both heart glad to be going home, but we have enjoyed our trip so much.

Remember us kindly to the Allans.

Yours sincerely,
L. M. Macdonald

The Leaskdale Letters
(letters from 1912 to 1925)

L. M. Montgomery resumes her correspondence with G. B. MacMillan after settling into the manse in Leaskdale, Ontario. Leaskdale becomes a home to her, and during the first four years there she has three children: Chester, Hugh Alexander (stillborn), and Stuart.

The Leaskdale years are L. M. Montgomery's most productive literarily, yet during them she experiences much worry and sorrow. In letters to MacMillan she agonizes over the battles of World War I; she is distressed by Ewen's frequent illnesses. The strongest and best letter, February 26, 1919, describes her anguish over the death of Fredericka Campbell, her dearest friend.

Visits to Prince Edward Island (1913, 1915, 1918, 1921, 1923, 1924) and trips to Muskoka (1922) and Kentucky (1924) renew her strength.

In 1923 she celebrates her friendship with MacMillan by dedicating her most autobiographical novel, Emily of New Moon, *to him. She also publishes during these years:* Chronicles of Avonlea *(1912),* The Golden Road *(1913),* Anne of the Island *(1915),* The Watchman & Other Poems *(1916),* Anne's House of Dreams *(1917),* Rainbow Valley *(1919),* Rilla of Ingleside *(1921), and* Emily Climbs *(1925).*

63

The Manse
Leaskdale, Ont.
Can.

January 20, 1912

Dear Mr. MacMillan:

I am going to make, not an apology, but a simple explanation, of my seemingly unconscionable delay in reply-
ing to your most welcome letter of October 30th. Ever
since arriving in Leaskdale, up to New Year's, I simply
could not, and did not write any letters except such as
absolutely had to be written. I was so busy "setting my
house in order," and receiving and returning calls, that
I had no time for anything else. I could get no maid and
consequently had all the housekeeping duties to attend
to myself. But now I have a good maid, my *house* is a
home, and I am at liberty to return to my old pursuits. I
have, with the joy of an exile returning home, taken up
my literary work again, and I am also getting back to old
delightful correspondences, which have lost nothing of
their former charm, and which I hope will not be interrupted in future for any length of time.

Firstly, due thanks for the delightful little book you
sent me at Xmas. It is charming all through. The picture
of that delightful, suggestive, tantalizing gate in the
frontispiece, is one of the dearest things I've seen for a
long time. I think I shall have to write a poem on it.

I sent you a little volume issued by our Canadian
Press Club, of which I am a Vice President. But it is not
the book I intended to send you. I went into Toronto in
December and got a copy of our Canadian poet's—Rob-
ert Service—"Songs of a Sourdough," which scored an
immense success a couple of years ago. The poems are
Klondike poems. But when I got home no such book
was to be found among my purchases—nor, for that
matter, has it ever turned up since. I must have lost it on

the street or in the throng around some Xmas counter. I tried to get another copy but all the nice ones were sold out and as time was getting very short I sent you "Canadian Days" instead.

I have had time to do hardly any reading since coming home, hardly even the papers, but now I hope to return to my good old habits in this respect also.

Leaskdale is a very pretty country place—would be almost as pretty as Cavendish if it had the sea—which by the way, I miss heart-breakingly at times. It is a farming settlement, so would not be marked on any map. We are only forty miles from Toronto. I find the people here nice and kind. Yes, I *like* Leaskdale very much. But as yet I do not *love* it. Perhaps I shall in time. But so far the only spot on earth I really *love* is that seaward looking slope where I lived and dreamed and worked for so many years. At times—generally in the winter twilight— I am very homesick and feel as if I would exchange all the kingdoms of the world and the glory thereof for a sunset ramble in Lover's Lane.

We have a nice brick manse, prettily situated, though too close to the other houses and backyards in the village to suit my love of solitude and retirement. We had a great deal of pleasure, as well as much hard work and some disappointments and vexations getting it fixed up, but now it is cosy and homelike. I love our library— where I hope to see you as a most welcome guest some day. The little plaque you sent in your letter adorns its walls, the gilt frame harmonizing admirably with the golden brown of the wall paper. But neither Mr. M. nor myself need any such reminder of the days we spent in Alloa and Berwick. They shine out in the memory of our trip like a special constellation and we can never forget the pleasant walks and talks we had in your old and lovely land.

Most of the photos I took turned out very well. The one of Homecliff Glen was a failure. I arranged them in my album the other day and all the memories connected with them came vividly back.

Who do you suppose arrived along one day in late November? Why his Royal Highness "Daffy," my big gray cat of old home days, *alias* the "Paddy" of the *Story Girl*. He was sent up from home by express in a box, with slats nailed over the top to allow access of air. I understand he protested vociferously against being thus "cabined, cribbed, and confined" at home and all the way to the station there. But he was three days and nights on the road, so I suppose his spirit was subdued, or his voice wore out before he got here, for he never uttered a squeak all the way from the station. When we took off the cover he climbed leisurely out and stretched himself. He was not at all hungry, having been well supplied with food when he left, but he was extremely thirsty and drank three saucers of milk and one of water without stopping. Then he climbed into my lap and kissed me as gravely and humanly as possible. He has been perfectly contented and happy ever since and is such company for us. He seems the only living link between me and the old life. Mr. *Mac.* spoils him worse than I do.

At present I am busy revising the best of my short stories as Mr. Page is going to bring a volume of them out in the spring. The title is to be "Chronicles of Avonlea," and the tales have to be rewritten to fit into Avonlea life and people. I don't care greatly for the task, but it will soon be done, and then I shall be free to attempt work more after my own heart— a second *Story Girl* volume. This, of course will not appear until 1913.

. . .

Mr. Mac. joins with me in wishing you a happy and prosperous New Year.

Yours most sincerely,
L. M. Montgomery Macdonald

The Manse
Leaskdale, Ont.

September 13, 1913

Dear Mr. MacMillan:
At last, in the busy, "hustling" existence that is my life at
present a quiet hour has come. I am all alone—Chester
boy[1] is asleep—and I can sit down and answer your letter, received so long ago that the date makes me
ashamed of myself. And yet why should I be ashamed? I
would have written sooner if I could. I *could not*; so on
the knees of the gods be the blame!

.   .   .

Your letter was written in April and mine, to which it
was an answer, in March. March and April seem many
moons ago to me. I seem to have "lived" so much and so
rapidly since then that they must have belonged to another year. We had a most beautiful spring—I never remember one quite so lovely. The spring is the time I like
best in the Ontario year. We certainly have beautiful
springs here—much more beautiful than in P.E.I.
where the springs are late and chilly, owing to the east
winds from the ice floes. P.E.I's summer and autumn
are much more lovely but Ontario scores with its
springs. How was your garden this year? Ours was—and
is—fine. But we lost much of its delight this summer by
being away most of its growing time. My aster beds are
resplendent now and make a deep glorious note of color
amid the mellow greens of the lawn.
My new book "The Golden Road" was finished in
May. I wrote the last ten chapters in a hurry and tur-
moil. Indeed, the whole book was written in odds and
ends of time and so left a disagreeable impression of
"unfinishedness" on my mind. Yet a friend told me yes-

1. Chester Cameron Macdonald (1912-1964) was born on July 7.

terday that it was my best book since Green Gables. I wonder if you will think so. It was published September 6th and I ordered a copy sent you. I am now girding up the loins of my mind to begin a third "Anne" book. This is to be written to satisfy my publisher and public, not myself. I am very reluctant to begin it. It seems so hard to get back into the *atmosphere* of *Anne*—like putting on a dress worn years ago, which, no matter how beautiful still, is something I have outgrown and find out of fashion with my later development. However, I shall make the attempt in order to win peace for myself. I fear that I must henceforth be a slave to the style that the public have learned to expect from me. They will not tolerate a change. And I should like to try my hand at a different type of book. Someday I *shall*—when I have made enough money to be independent of the public taste.

Of course the great event of my summer was my visit "home." I had looked forward to it for two years—and now it is over. But I certainly had a glorious time while it lasted. I left for the Island the first of July and did not return till the 20th of August.

I shall never forget my first glimpse of the sea again. It was the morning after our arrival on the good old red soil. Of course we had crossed the strait the evening before but it had been rainy and cold and dark so I had not really seen it. But the morning was glorious. We left town for a drive in the fresh sunshine and the bracing air. We drove to the crest of a long red hill and—there was the sea. I was not prepared for the flood of emotion which swept over me when I saw it. I was stirred to the very deeps of my being—tears filled my eyes—I trembled! For a moment it seemed passionately to me that I could *never* leave it again.

We visited Mr. M's people and then I went to Park Corner—where we were married—for ten days. We had some beautiful drives over the Island roads. There are no such roads in Ontario. We have beautiful roads here—and beautiful landscapes. But they want the indefinable charm that haunts—and is the very soul—of the P.E.I. roads and scenes.

I have often tried to define the difference but I can never think I have succeeded. It is too elusive—too subtle. Is it the touch of austerity in the Island landscapes that gives it its distinctive beauty? And whence comes this austerity? Is it from the fir and spruce? Or the glimpses of the sea? Or does it go deeper, to the very soul of the land? For lands have personalities, as have human beings.

Most of our drives were in the evenings—such beautiful evenings, dewy, cool, and fragrant, with fairy tints in the western sky. And as we drove along everywhere we breathed the delicious scent of dying fir. I had not smelled it since I left home. Of all the fragrances the world over there is none like the odor of fir distilled on dew-damp twilight air. And there is no more exquisite sight than a field of ox-eye daisies in that same twilight. To be sure, those same ox-eye daisies are pestiferous weeds and their presence is an evidence of bad farming. But for airy fairy grace and charm there is naught to match a sunset field of them.

From Park Corner I went to Cavendish and spent three weeks there—three beautiful weeks, with a vein of sadness running through them. It seemed so strange to be in Cavendish and not be in the old home. It is closed up now and I went not near it—I could not bear to. But one evening in the dusk I went to a hill that commanded a view of it and looked down upon it—and I saw it, and the window of my old room where I once sat and dreamed and wrote, and I saw the old orchards and the old lane and the old woods I loved. And I went back from that pilgrimage to shrines forsaken and altars overthrown with a very full heart.

My first week was spent on the farm on which is Lover's Lane. And I haunted it by day and night. 'Twas as beautiful as ever. And I went to the old shore and had some glorious "dips." And I picked wild strawberries in the old meadows and spruce gum in the woods—and presently it seemed as if I had never been away from Cavendish and as if my Ontario home was a dream from which I had awakened. I was very glad to come back to it. I grew tired "living in a trunk" and I was thankful enough after three days of strenuous travel to reach my own fireside once again. Since coming home I have been exceedingly busy, picking up dropped threads and doing a thousand and one things.

.   .   .

I must close now, for it is nearing dinner time. I shall look forward to your letter with interest. Wales is a country of which I seem to know nothing. Mr. M. sends regards and good wishes. So do I.

Yours sincerely,
L. M. Macdonald

The Manse
Leaskdale, Ont.

October 16, 1914

Dear Mr. MacMillan:

I have mislaid my correspondence notebook so I do not know exactly what the date of my last letter to you was. But I know it was too long ago. I should have answered your letter many weeks ere this, but somehow it seemed impossible. Part of the time, I have been ill; part of it too busy and all the time too worried and anxious to write letters. "Our world has passed away in wanton over-throw."

But this dull, windy, drizzling autumn afternoon I have sat down at my desk, resolved to make an attempt at last to pick up the dropped threads again.

It seems a hundred years since I wrote you last. It *is* a hundred years if we "count time by heart throbs." Terrible as all the things that have happened since then my own personal sorrow seems the blackest of all to me. On August 13th a little son[1] was born to us—dead! I cannot write of it. The grief and disappointment almost killed me. No one but a mother, and a mother who has had a similar bereavement can understand what it meant to me. All the sorrow of my life before put together could not equal it in agony.

I was long in recovering my strength, and though I am pretty well now physically I have not recovered from the shock mentally. It seems as if something had *broken* in my spirit. Everything seems changed. No doubt the dread and shadow of this awful war hanging over us contributes to this feeling.

For oh, is it not hideous—unbelievable—unthinkable! What must it be to you who are so near it! It seemed to break over the world like a thundercloud. Europe was in flames from end to end before we could realize what had happened. Oh, surely surely Germany cannot win! If she does I shall give up all faith in a guiding Providence. These past ten days, when the news seemed bad or dubious, have weighed on me like a nightmare. Some nights I cannot sleep, especially after reading of the atrocities committed in Belgium. It is no joke but a simple fact that I have not had one decent *dinner* since the war began. Our dinner hour is one. The mail comes in at 12.30. If the news is good it excites me, if it is bad it upsets me and I can eat little. While if I decide to exert all my will power and refuse to look at the papers until after dinner the suspense is worst of all and I can eat absolutely nothing. When I tell this to our comfortable, stolid country people who, from a happy combination

1. Hugh Alexander.

71

of ignorance and lack of imagination, do not seem to *realize* the war at all, they laugh as if they thought I was trying to be funny. Those who perceive that I am in earnest think I am crazy. To-day the war news is a shade brighter. That is why I am writing you. If it had not been I would not have had enough "grit" to begin a letter.

Thank you muchly for those *Daily Sketches* and *Mirrors* you send. Always interesting they are tenfold so now. Yet they are ironical enough. Their exultation over victories that have since been eclipsed, their glumness over defeats that have since been avenged, sound almost amusing by the time they get here!

Truly, time brings about curious reversals—Japan and Russia allies—England fighting with France. Russia seems to be doing good work. The reports we get from the eastern arena are horribly confused and contradictory. Your card came today, stating that you had been planting bulbs extensively. Evidently you do not expect a Zeppelin to drop a bomb in your garden. Is the Zeppelin menace considered seriously in Britain? What a change there must be over there since those pleasant summer days when we rambled about Berwick and dreamed of "battles long ago." Now, the battles of today eclipse all else.

What do you think of Kipling's war poem? Perhaps it is not much as to literature—certainly not comparable to "Recessional" or "Hymn before Action." But there is a certain bare, stark strength in it which seems to me to accord well with the grimness of the struggle. And he has not lost his knack of expressing the public state of mind in a few pithy words. "Our world has passed away in wanton overthrow"—and "Comfort content, delight, the ages slow-bought gain, They vanished in a night"— seem to me to express exactly what I felt on the day war was declared. Whatever is the outcome of the war the world can never be the same again. Pitt said after Austerlitz—"Roll up the map of Europe it will not be wanted these twenty years." The old map of Europe will never be wanted again.

Yet I believe the capture of Antwerp and Ostend mark the highest point of the German successes. Hereafter their tide will ebb. I may be mistaken. Before you read this letter events may have occurred that will render me a false prophet. I believe they are making one huge final effort to break through to Paris. *If* the Allies can force them back again the invasion of France will be over. If *not*—!!!!!!

I want to stop writing about the war and turn to other things; I shall not be able to do so totally. Probably all through this letter I shall revert to it as ideas occur to me. But I shall at least make an effort to discuss other matters—yea, even matters literary.

I am at work on a new *Anne* book—to be called *Anne of Redmond* and deal with the four years of *Anne's* college course. At no time did I take any great interest in it for I never wanted to write it. And now it seems to me all but impossible to sit calmly down and write for schoolgirls and their little doings while the nations are locked in their death struggle. There, you see I am back to the war already!! But it is true. And so the new book won't amount to anything except in the eyes of schoolgirls, who insist on knowing what further happened to Anne and Gilbert. Such as it is I hope to have it finished and out of the way by Christmas. But much may intervene to delay it. On days when the war news is bad I simply cannot write at all.

I suppose the British book market is pretty well knocked out by the war? The Canadian book market is seriously affected, the American to some degree. As an illustration of how war to-day affects even neutral nations the U.S. treasury has a deficit of one hundred millions because of the war and has to put on a special tax to make it good.

Sunday, October 18.

.   .   .

I have written a letter stained through with the hues of the war. I dare not ask you to reply soon. Yet I would be so glad if you could and tell me all about the state of affairs and feeling there. It is possible this letter may never get to you—it may fall into the way of a German cruiser. But thank God England is *still* mistress of the seas. I cannot believe but that she will remain so. Yet those German fiends stick at nothing.

The last word shall *not* be of war. Instead it shall be of cheer and hope and good wishes.

Yours sincerely,
L. M. Macdonald

St. Paul's Manse
Leaskdale, Ont.

August 2, 1915

Dear Mr. MacMillan:

.   .   .

You began your letter in April. It seems a century since then. If we "should count time by heart-throbs" I, and I suppose all thinking people have lived several eons since this day year. For a year I have not wakened one morning without miserably asking "What will be the war news to-day?" For a year I have never seen my husband going out for the mail without a horrible sinking of the heart and a dread of his return. Lately, it has been so terrible—this German sweep against Russia. And *nothing* elsewhere to offset it. *What* are the Allies doing? *Why* is it that they have seemingly been able to make no effort where they should have made most. It is a sickening query. It seems to me that the situation is more critical than it has been ever since the Germans were so near Paris. Canada seems in a veritable war-flame. We are awake to the seriousness of the situation at last. But is it in time? At all events it is certain that we are in for another winter of war, with all the strain that implies. Thank God that at least the Russian army has so far escaped destruction and it seems that it probably will. What I fear most from the fall of Warsaw is the effect on the wavering Balkans and a renewed and terrific German onslaught in the west. But we can only wait and see. If only the Allies could force the Dardanelles: But that seems a hopeless task. I fear they blundered terribly at the outset, trying to force the strait by warships alone. My only hope is in Kitchener and Lloyd George. I believe they will save the situation if anybody can.

Now for your letter: I am indeed glad that "The Alhambra" opened to you the same world it has always opened to me. Wherein consists the indefinable charm of the book? It cannot be altogether in the style for, although Irving's style is delightful, none of his other books, much as I love them and great as is my pleasure in them, give me the same peculiar delight as does the *Alhambra*. The special charm must consist in style and subject combined. The one is in perfect harmony with the other. One does not *read* the book; one *lives* it. When I open its covers I always feel a peculiar sensation, as if I had stepped through an enchanted gateway and it had shut behind me, shutting out the real prosaic world and shutting me in "the land where dreams come true." It is one of my dearest wishes some day to visit the Alhambra. And yet—would it be wise? I question if it would really be to me the fairy castle of Irving's book and then I should be so much the poorer by reason of a lost ideal.

.   .   .

I suppose the Zeppelin raids keep the inhabitants of
Britain rather uncomfortable. But from a military point
of view they have certainly been failures. Nothing they
have done has had the slightest effect from a military
point of view, so they must have been a disappointment
to the German Staff which expected such wonders of
them.

No, Kipling's poem did not reach me, so something
must have happened to it. Never mind, I'll likely get another copy ere long. It is often reprinted in Canadian
papers.

"Anne of the Island" is out at last. It was to have been
published by the first of June. But the printers could
not get the colored inset and frontispiece ready in time
because they had always before got the ink *from Germany*
and this time they had to experiment with home-made
productions and it was some time before they could get
inks that would suit. I instructed my publishers to send
you a copy and I hope you got it safely.

.   .   .

Oh, that Lusitania atrocity! It was hideous—hellish!
Those drowned babies! The thought of them haunted
me for weeks. I was going in to Toronto that night when
the news came. Never shall I forget Yonge St. the next
morning. It is the thronged business street of Toronto
and everyone had an issue of the morning paper and
read it as he or she went along, running into people and
being run into, and taking no heed. There were so
many Toronto people on board that the city was stirred
to its depths. The United States went mad over the subject—but they can do nothing. They are even less prepared for war than England was and Germany knows
it.

I think my last letter to you was written in February. It
seems a very long time since then. In March I had a trying fortnight. I got a telegram from the General Hospi-

tal, Montreal saying that my cousin Frede Campbell[1] was so ill with typhoid that she was not expected to live. I do not know if I have ever mentioned Frede to you. She and I have been more to each other than most sisters all our lives, and the news of her illness was a dreadful shock. I rushed at once to Montreal. Nobody had any hope of her when I arrived there. I could not face a world with no Frede in it. A dreadful week followed. Every morning when I wakened I expected to hear that Frede was dying. But she pulled through after all. Inch by inch the tide turned and she rallied back to life. Never have I felt so utterly thankful. I stayed with her until she was out of danger, then came home, rather done up by the strain of those two weeks. Then in May I had a bad time myself for nearly a fortnight with ulcerating teeth. The first of June I went down home and stayed until the 20th of July. In many ways it was enjoyable; but on the whole my visit home was a disappointment. The weather was bad; it rained almost every day of three weeks; changes had come; a young friend died suddenly while I was home under tragic circumstances; my own health was not very good; and finally the bad— unvaringly bad—war news damped the pleasure of everything. I was glad to get back to my own roof tree again—though it has rained almost every day since I came. Rain pursues me this summer. If there is a drouth anywhere they should send for me.

This letter has taken many days and sittings; and the Germans have got Warsaw; and still, still, still the Allies do *nothing*, anywhere. What will the outcome be? I dread the autumn.

I enclose a couple of snaps of Chester and some clip-

---

1. Fredericka Elmanstine Campbell (1883-1919), was the youngest member of the John and Annie Campbell family of Park Corner, and L.M.'s first cousin. In 1911, L.M. dedicated *The Story Girl* to her; and in 1921, *Rilla of Ingleside.*

pings that may interest you. I think the poem "Memories" a very beautiful one.

Mr. Mac. sends kind regards. With all good wishes

Yours sincerely,

L. M. Macdonald

The Manse
Leaskdale, Ont.

April 7, 1918

Dear Mr. MacMillan:

You would have had this letter by this time if Hindenburg had not broken the British line at St. Quentin a fortnight ago to-day—March 24th. I shall *never* forget the date—I went to church in the morning. Before doing so I took your letters out of the "unanswered" pigeon hole of my secretary and laid them on my desk. "This afternoon," I said to Mr. Macdonald, "I am going to write to Mr. MacMillan."

I went to church in a fairly calm frame of mind, although the news of the great offensive had come on Friday. In a way it was almost a relief. We had been waiting so long cringing like a dog before an expected blow, for the tempest to burst. Now it had come and in a few days it would be over, one way or another. I firmly believed it would be over "our way." On March 1st I had had another of my strange dreams. I have had nine since the war broke out and *every one* has come true. This time I dreamed that I held a newspaper in my hand and a great black headline ran across it. "There are 30 evil days in store for us." I awoke, believing that the German offensive would come in March and be ended practically by March 31st. But *how* ended? It did not seem to me that my dream foretold that. I worried all day more or less over the question. That night I dreamed again. I thought I stood on a great plain, blood-red in the sunset and I held in my arms a man whose face I could not see but whom I knew to be dying. As I held him he died, and fell from my arms to the ground. Then I saw his face—and it was the face of the Kaiser's *father*—the man whom I had known in my girlhood as the "Crown Prince of Germany" and whose pictured face was very familiar to me as he dragged through the long months of his fatal illness. I wakened from that dream, believing that the coming offensive would end in defeat, if not disaster, to the House of Hohenzollern.

On Saturday the news seemed quite favorable. The line seemed to be holding in spite of the terrible onset. I came home from church and began to prepare dinner, my maid being away. Presently the telephone bell rang and Mr. M. went to it. He came out a few minutes later. His face was positively gray.

"There is a message from Toronto," he said. "The British line is broken and the German guns are raining shells on Paris."

Mr. MacMillan I shall never forget the agony of that moment. I cringe even yet as I think of it. Remember we knew nothing of the long-range gun. We thought that the Germans must be at the very gates of Paris and therefore that the British must have given way everywhere. Oh, what an afternoon that was! I was alone with the children[1] and I walked the floor. I could not read or rest or sleep or eat. The night seemed an endless agony. When the mail came Monday, the truth, bad as it really was, seemed good news compared to what we had heard. The line had been broken in one place only, the British were retreating in good order, and the Germans were still a long way from Paris. We passed two more days in miserable suspense and then the word came that the offensive was checked. The good news continued and on April 1st—just 20 days after my dream—the

1. A third son, Ewan Stuart, was born on October 7, 1915.

pronouncement was that the "first phase" of the offensive was over, and all the Germans had gained for the blood they had poured out was a few wrecked miles of barren territory.

I believe it is all they *will* gain. I believe the worst is over, whatever is yet to come. But never, in all the years of eternity, will I forget that Sunday of March 24th.

.   .   .

We had an election here last December. We have had many elections before but never one like this. The whole country was convulsed. The issue, of course, was conscription. I had a vote, because of my soldier brother,[2] and so infected was I with the prevailing excitement that I actually "took the stump" and made two speeches in Toronto on "Women's Responsibility in the Election." When election day came I polled my first vote—and felt just about the same afterwards as before. The Union Gov't swept the country and conscription came into force. They are having great trouble in Quebec though. Co-incident with the opening of the German offensive riots broke out in Quebec City, resulting in much bloodshed and the city is now under martial law. I have not a doubt that German gold was at the bottom of it. And was not that Halifax Disaster awful? I knew Halifax so well. I lived there two years—was there if you remember, when our correspondence began. I have many friends there. None of them were killed but some were terribly injured. They say the pilot of the *Imo* was a German and I shall never believe but what the Germans were responsible for it. What horrors have been in the world since the *Titanic* went down! Speaking of my poor brother, he had his leg blown off at Vimy

2. Hugh Carlyle Montgomery, son of Hugh John Montgomery and Mary Ann McRae. L.M.'s two half brothers and two half sisters were Katie, Bruce, Carlyle, and Ila May.

Ridge and was sent home last fall. He has been all winter in Toronto and is now getting his artificial leg in place. Poor chap, he is so cheery and plucky and can tell such capital tales of trench life.

You were asking what I recited at the recruiting meetings—which of course have ceased since conscription came in. Well, I had lots of pieces, mostly patriotic of course. But the one I always gave for an encore was "In Flanders Fields," written by one of our Canadian soldiers, who now himself sleeps "somewhere in France." The poem has had a tremendous success. It was reprinted everywhere and likely you have seen it but I enclose a copy on the chance that you have not. I think it very fine. It was a regular slogan here in the election campaign.

.   .   .

Vale, my friend. Amid all the wreck of matter and the crash of worlds the friendship of "kindred spirits" at least abides. May the gods be good to you.

Yours sincerely,
L. M. Macdonald

The Manse
Leaskdale, Ont.

Feb 26, 1919

Dear Mr. MacMillan:

Your letter was written on June 30; there have been several notes and cards since then; many bundles of papers; and a couple of Christmas books. None has been acknowledged. Yet I do not feel at all guilty or apologetic. Nor, I think, will you consider that I should feel so when you hear the history of the past year. The sorrow, the worry, the mental and physical suffering which has been my lot during the past five months have not been equalled by all the previous years of my life put together. But I will begin where I left off in my last letter and take everything in its course, merely remarking that Mr. Macdonald and my two boys are quite well and that the bereavements that have changed life for me have not been in my home.

The earliest unanswered note I have of yours is one dated Ap13/18. It accompanied *Punch* with your "Black Flower of a Blameless Life," which was excellently good and holds a place of honor in my scrapbook. (In passing, I intend to try to get a full set of Punch from the opening of the war to the close. I think I can manage it through the Tract Society of Toronto. It would certainly be worth having.) The *Gazette* which you sent containing the review of *Anne's House of Dreams* also came. A clipping bureau also sent me the *Spectator* one, and the *British Weekly* had another equally kind. Your verses on "Weapon Week" enclosed with this note were good of their kind, too. The person who added the extra verse isn't as good a rhymster as you—unless he meant "got" to be pronounced very Scotchily indeed.

Now, for your letter of June 30th. It was written when the German hosts were still pouring Westward. Oh, last spring! What a horror it was! I think I wrote you in my last letter of dreaming early in March that I saw in a newspaper a head line "Thirty Evil Days are Coming," and then the next night that I held a dying man who, when he fell from my hold dead I recognized as the Kaiser's father, the man whom I knew in my girlhood as the Crown Prince Frederick. Well, that dream sustained me amid all the opening hours of the offensive until the 20th of April was past. Then when reverse still followed reverse I gave up all faith in my dreams. Later on, in June, I dreamed again that I saw Marshall Foch and he said simply "October 3rd." At the time, I paid little significance to it, having, as aforesaid, lost faith in my dreams. But when the tide turned and the second "miracle of the Marne" took place I thought of those dreams again—because it was the *Crown Prince's* army that first met defeat. Well, I got out my notebook and I counted up the days from the 21st of March to the day Foch struck at the German flank on which the news had been positively bad—when the Germans had made some advance big or little. *There were exactly thirty days.* On all the other days they had been checked. You can make what you like of that! But *I* said, to my cousin at Park Corner, when I was home, "The tide has turned *for good.* There will be no more reverses. The star of the Hohenzollerns has set for ever." Was it not a strange thing that the Germans reached and crossed the Marne again—and that they made the very same mistake they made before—of exposing their flank?

Do you, over there, *realize* that the war is over? Somehow, I haven't *sensed* it yet. It had come to seem our normal state. I was down home in P.E.I. on a sorrowful errand, when the news of the armistice came—on a quiet, remote North Shore farm. There was no celebration there; but everywhere else people went mad. Even here in Leaskdale they had a bonfire and burned the Kaiser in effigy. What a downfall was his! Have you ever read Byron's "Ode to Napoleon Bonaparte"? If not, read it and note how two thirds of its stanzas might have been addressed to the Kaiser with hardly the change of a word, especially the one ending,

"All quelled: Hark spirit, what must be
The madness of thy memory?"

The war is over; but the problems it has left will furnish our great-grand-children with occupation. And what of my dream of "October 3rd"? Well, this is one of the things that cannot be proved. But here is what I believe.

You may remember that on October 4 Prince Maximilian announced before the German Reichstag that it had been decided to ask for an armistice. That announcement was made on the *fourth*. Does it not seem reasonable to suppose that the *decision* to ask for an armistice was made on the *third*? I shall believe that until the contrary is proved.

Do you find life and newspapers a little *flat* since the war ended? Nobody I feel sure, could have been more profoundly thankful than I was that it was ended. But after being accustomed for four years to horrors, alarms, terrible reverses or splendid victories, stimulated to the last notch of endurance—well, when all this suddenly ceased, ordinary existence seemed fearfully *tasteless* and monotonous. To open a newspaper without trembling with dread of what one might see—it was blessed but it was tame!!

How do you like "daylight saving"? We had it here last summer for the first. The towns and villages were quite enthusiastic about it but the farmers are bitterly opposed to it for the most part. One of the current jokes last summer was that a certain old farmer met a friend on the road and asked him what time it was. "Nine o'clock," was the reply. "Oh, but is that God's time or Borden's time?" was the suspicious question.

Personally I liked it well enough but found it impossible to get the children to bed by "Borden's time" as it was broad daylight! We found it inconvenient because so many of our people, who are farmers, would not put the clocks on. When we went anywhere to visit we always had to find out what time they went by, because we are always supposed to go to supper and it is embarrassing to arrive an hour before you are expected or wanted!

One thing I did like—when eleven o'clock came and I had a very interesting book half read it was quite nice to think "Oh, it's only ten o'clock really. I can read another hour"!!!

Last spring we invested in an automobile—a five pas-

senger Chevrolet. We had intended to wait until the war
was over but our old buggy went "completely bust" so
we got the car. Cars are as thick as hops here. All the
farmers have made so much money during the war that
they can all afford them. We found ours very convenient all summer for long distance travelling. I have not
learned to run it yet—don't think I'll ever have the
nerve to. I content myself with poking Mr. Mac. in the
back with my parasol if I think he is going more than 20
miles, and saying, "Beware" in a sepulchral tone when I
see him preparing to turn a corner. Do you remember
that car ride we had—with Miss Allen—while we were at
Berwick, when we ran over but did not hurt a dog? *We*
ran over and killed one on Yonge St. this summer. It
spoiled the day for me—I was haunted by the cries of
the poor animal. It was in no way our fault and it might
have overturned the car but I felt as if we were guilty of
murder!

But I don't know that I am wholly pleased with cars.
Personally, I prefer a buggy with a nice lovable *living*
horse. I occasionally remember with regret the old
days—and moonlit nights—buggy driving.

Anyhow, I'm glad *my* courting days were over before
the cars came!! There is no romance whatever in a car.
A man can't safely drive it with one arm! And loitering
is impossible.

What do you think of the Bolskeviks? There is a terrible spirit of unrest in the world, call it by what name you
will. The U.S. is seething with it under the lid. Do you
know, I think the world will *slump* for a while—twenty or
thirty years. It will be just like a person after a terrible
strain, spineless and nerveless for a certain time.

By the way, did you see the "new" star last June which
so vastly excited the astronomical world? I caught a
glimpse of it one night. The opinion of astronomers, I
believe, was that it was the product of a collision which
occurred in the time of Moses. But even this event could

not dwarf for me into what may be the proper perspective in sidereal affairs the fact that the Germans were once again near Paris!

I have never had time to resume my studies in astronomy which so fascinated me a year or so before my marriage. I am afraid I never shall. I should have liked to have been an astronomer—failing that, to have a few astronomers among my acquaintances. Fancy talking the gossip of the hosts of heaven! I wonder if astronomers feel much interest in earthly affairs. Perhaps a student of the canals of Mars would not be so keenly awake to the significance of a few yards or so of trenches lost or won on the Western front. By some curious kink of "the law of association of ideas" this reminds me that not long ago I read somewhere that Ernest Renan wrote his Life of Jesus during the siege of Paris in 1870 and "enjoyed doing it very much." I suppose we could call him a philosopher! I have also read that just before his death he said that his only regret was that he could not live long enough to see what "that extremely interesting young man, the German Emperor would do in his career." If Ernest Renan "walks" to-day and sees what that "interesting young man" has done to his beloved France, not to speak of the world, I wonder if his mental detachment is as complete as it was in 1870.

The middle of June I went down to P. E. Island for a visit and took my two lads. I had not been down for three years. I stayed until the first of August and had a very delightful time—so delightful that I felt at the time that I was in debt to the Powers That Wait for it and would have to pay. I shall never again have such a happy vacation in the homeland. What has happened since will always mean a constant heartache in any visit home. I spent three weeks in Cavendish. Most of this time the weather was charming; but the first Sunday after my arrival we had a cold driving rainstorm from the east. And I revelled in it. It was so thoroughly "downeastern." We never have anything like it in Ontario. The Ontario rains are often heavy enough but they have no "bite" to them—no such fine real fury and tang. Then in the evening it cleared up goldenly and I went for a ride in a friend's big "Overland." For the motor car is on the Island at last—to stay!

In one way I'm rather pleased. I have hated to hear the Island made fun of for its prejudice against motor cars. On the other hand I resent their presence in that haunt of ancient peace. I wanted it kept sacred to the gods of the old time. I wanted to think that there was one place in the world where the strident honk-honk of the car horn could never jar on the scented air.

But I enjoyed my drive in my friend's car for all that—even if we did get ingloriously ditched at the end, owing to a certain grim old dame who *wouldn't* rein her horse out to let us pass. The others were furious, but in my heart I believe I sympathized with the old girl. Had I been a spinster lady driving along behind my own nag, in maiden meditation fancy free, I believe *I* wouldn't have stirred a finger either when some obstreperous car honked behind me. No, I should just have sat up as dourly as she did and said "Take the ditch or the devil for all of ye."

It all depends on the point of view.

On the evening I arrived in Cavendish I got a blow in the face. All the old "school woods" had been cut down. That once wide green beautiful hill of plumy spruce and fir was now an abomination of desolation of stumps. The schoolhouse sat on its crest wantonly, indecently naked. The whole sight was obscene. If I had had the power I would have spitted the author of the outrage on a bayonet without fear and without remorse. He had the soul of a Hun.

Seriously, it hurt me horribly. A thousand pitiful little ghosts were robbed of their haunt by the felling of those trees. Scores of tender memories were outraged and banished. Why, my first sweetheart had said "I love you" to me under those trees. And now such a desecration!

But no wickedness was worked in Lover's Lane. It was as lovely as ever—and the Island more lovely. I had not somehow remembered that the sea was so blue, the roads so red and the wood-nooks so ferny and green and fairy-haunted. Yes, the fairies still abide there. Even the motor cars cannot chase them away. Scores of them lived, I am persuaded, in the white and pink bells of the columbines that grew wild in the old orchard of the place where I stayed.

I spent many days at the shore, lying on the sand and dreaming as I thought I had forgot to dream, while the boys paddled in the Atlantic. Or perhaps I climbed to the top of the old "Watch-Tower" and repeated, as I always did when standing on it,

"Could I but climb where Moses stood
And view the landscape o'er."

The "Watch Tower" was the largest and highest dune of the sand-hills and the view from it is, I believe, the most beautiful and *satisfying*—at least to me—that I have ever beheld. I gazed at it, not only with physical eyes, seeing material beauty, but with the eyes of memory which saw all that in the past had filled it with charm for me. I could see from it almost everything in Cavendish that I ever loved—the old church hill and graveyard, the school, the woods that held Lover's Lane, the old red roads, the two ponds, the Shore Lane, my own old home site, the lovely New London harbor and New London Point, the shining sandshore, the red rock shore and the sweep of azure sea.

One evening I spent wandering about the graveyard where so many of my dead lie. It was not a sorrowful tryst. I felt very happy and among friendly presences. I felt again acutely the peculiar, indefinable charm of P. E. Island. A certain wellspring of fancy which I thought had gone dry in me bubbled up as freshly as of old.

Moreover, there was one little thing which made it seem marvellously like old times. Years ago, whenever I walked there in the evening the clear calm air was always threaded by the distant sounds of children's voices and laughter at Uncle John's. In recent years there has been silence for those children had grown up and gone. But on this evening of which I write the olden music sounded again—this time from the manse where Chester and Stuart were playing and calling merrily with Doris and Ian Stirling.

"So generations in their course decay,
So flourish these when those have passed away."

On another twilight I crept across the fields to my old home. It was a sad sight. The old maple grove was gone and most of the old birches. How sorrowful, how forlorn the old house looked.

I slipped around to the back and saw that the door was secured only by a wire easily unfastened. I did what I had never expected to do again—I opened the door and once more crossed the old threshold. I stood in the old kitchen. It was quite clearly visible in the dusk. A damp odor of decaying plaster hung heavy on the air. I went through the sitting room and the parlor. In each I shut my eyes and *thought myself* back into the past. Everything was around me as of old—each picture, each chair, each book or flower in its old place. I went up the dark stairs. I stood on the threshold of my old room— my old small illimitable kingdom where I had written my books long ago. But I did not go in. The window was boarded up and the room was as dark as midnight. Somehow I could not enter it. It was too full of ghosts— lonely, hungry ghosts. They would have pulled me in among them and kept me. I would have disappeared forever from the land of living men and nobody would ever have known what had become of me!

Then I went down and out and away. These pilgrimages to shadow land are eerie things with an uncanny sweetness. I think I will make no more of them.

The last two weeks of my stay I spent at Aunt Annie's at Park Corner. You will remember I was married from there. It was always a second home to me. Aunt Annie was like a mother—her son and her three daughters[1] like brother and sisters to me. Especially between her youngest daughter, Frede, and me has there been a long and wonderful friendship. Frede was there while I was and we had a beautiful holiday together. We were girls again. How we laughed! What delightful walks and prowls we had. And, though we knew it not, it was for the last time! One day at Park Corner an odd thing happened.

I never like to sit down thirteen at a table. My *reason* tells me that the superstition, like all superstitions is absurd. Something more primitive than reason insists on being uneasy. Sixteen years or so ago I was one of thirteen at a table and one of the thirteen died before six weeks had passed. I never again happened to sit thirteen at table again till this day at Park Corner. There was such a gang of us there, especially children that we never all sat down to a meal at once. Aunt Annie, Frede or Ella (George's wife) would wait on the table and eat afterwards. This day it happened that everyone sat down and I began to count merely out of curiosity to see how many were seated at the long table—George, Ella, Aunt Annie, John Cole (a neighbor), myself, Frede, Doris, Amy, Jim, Georgie, Maudie,[2] Chester and Stuart—*thirteen*!

More for a joke than anything else I said "Why, there are thirteen at the table."

1. George Campbell (1881-1918), Clara (1877-1932), Stella (1879-1955), and Fredericka (1883-1919).
2. Doris Stirling; Amy, Jim, Georgie, and Maudie are the children of George and Ella Johnstone Campbell (1876-1955).

The next moment I thought "Well, what an asinine thing of me to say. Here is Ella, expecting a baby and depressed and pessimistic as it is. If she believes in the 13 superstition it may prey on her mind and have a disastrous effect." To erase such impression from Ella's mind I laughed and said to Frede. "Frede, you were the thirteenth to sit down. The omen must be for you." Frede, had, however jumped up and declared she would not sit any longer. George, who it seemed, had never heard of the superstition laughed at her and called her a goose. The matter passed out of our minds. We did not really *believe* the legend and any lingering uneasiness vanished when Ella's little daughter[3] arrived a few days later.

But *three* of those who sat at that fatal table have since died—George himself, his little son Georgie, and—Frede.

I came home early in August. Aunt Annie came with me for a little visit. I found your letter awaiting me here and decided that I would answer it promptly. But I could not do so as long as Aunt Annie was here for all my spare time was devoted to giving her a good time. We motored her all over the country. I took her into the Toronto Exhibition and while there we went to see the famous British propaganda movie "Hearts of the World." Have you seen it? It is a wonderful thing. I was especially interested in it because a battle in which my brother Carl took part was featured in it—the battle of Courcelette—though it is not called by that name in the play. He had told us he recognized one scene in particular by a big round hole in a brick wall. So through all the play Aunt Annie and I watched for that hole. Holes there were without number but none seemed just to measure up to our expectations. Near the end came the hole—unmistakably *the* hole; and we both exclaimed

3. Georgie Fredericka MacFarlane Campbell.

aloud "Oh, there's the hole," much to the amusement of those in our vicinity.

This reminds me of a funny thing a friend told me. She went to see the movie. In one scene a girl, locked in a room, secretes a huge butcher knife in her stocking—or belt?—to protect herself. Enters a brutal German. In the ensuing struggle my friend got so excited over the seeming reality of the thing that she forgot she was not looking at a genuine struggle. She thought the girl must have forgotten her knife, so she suddenly stood up and shrieked aloud, so that she was heard all over the theatre, "The knife is in your stocking—the knife is in your stocking!" To add to the effect, the words had no sooner left her lips, than the girl pulled the knife and stabbed the German!

In one of the bundles of papers you sent me last summer I found a *most* interesting and intriguing "bit." It was on the Problems page in a prize essay on "Wallpapers I have known," signed "Quinceux." One sentence in it struck me—"wallpapers that came out or retreated when you looked at them with the right kind of eyes."

When I was a very small child—at latest before I was seven years old—I made a certain discovery. This was that if I looked at the paper on the wall of a room in a certain way I could cause that paper to appear in miniature before me, as if on a transparent screen floating in the air between me and the real wall. As for the "certain way" of looking, I don't know what it was like, naturally not being able to see my eyes in the process. But it seemed to me that I made a certain contraction of the muscles of the eyes which produced the "mirage." Once the "mirage" was produced my eyes seemed to revert to their normal condition and I could look at and see the mirage without anymore *conscious* effort than if I were looking at the real wall behind it. I could see the mirage as long as I looked at it but if I looked away it vanished. I could also cause it to vanish by another little movement of my eyes—a movement which did not seem strong enough to call a contraction—more of a "letting go," so to speak. I could cause the mirage to appear at any distance from the wall I liked—a foot out—half way across the room—a few inches from my eyes. The stronger the contraction the nearer it came. But I could also bring it near by a series of easy contractions. That is, I would cause it to appear a foot from the wall. Then, by looking at this mirage itself not at the wall, and making the movement of my eyes, I could bring it a foot or so nearer and so on, until I brought it as near as possible. The first mirage would be only a trifle smaller in pattern than the real paper. But with every advance it became smaller until the last one hung before my eyes the tiniest reproduction imaginable. These mirages were transparent, that is the real walls could be seen through them and yet they seemed perfectly solid and real. All through my childhood this was a favorite amusement of mine. I loved to produce those aerial wallpapers with their fancy roses and wreaths. The prettier the pattern, the prettier the result of course. Pictures or anything hanging on the wall were reproduced with it but I could not reproduce a picture by looking at it directly, or anything but paper.

I hadn't tried to do it for at least fifteen years. But when I read this essay in the *Gazette* I tried again and found that I still possessed the power, though I fancied it was a trifle harder to produce the result.

I have never come across any person who could do this or who seemed to have the faintest understanding of what I was talking about if I mentioned it. But I fancy this "Quinceux," whoever he or she may be, possesses it. If I can get time to think I shall write a letter to "Q" in care of the *Gazette* and see if I can find out.

Aunt Annie went home the first week in October and I went with her as far as Toronto. The Spanish flu was raging there then and scores were dying daily from it. You speak of having it and you also refer to it as a "Satanic influence." Your phrase is inspired. It was Satanic. It has ravaged Canada like a cyclone and though the top crest of the epidemic has passed it is very prevalent still. In the last 3 months of 1918, 7000 people died of it in Ontario alone. I have not the figures for the rest of Canada but in Toronto and Montreal the graves were dug by steam shovels,—large trenches were dug and the dead bodies placed in rows in them, many of them uncoffined, as coffins could not be obtained soon enough. However, when I went to Toronto matters had not come to this stage. The people were only beginning to get alarmed and were besieging the drug stores in hundreds trying to get preventives. After I had seen Aunt Annie off I came home. That evening I began to sneeze. The next day I came down with flu.

I was a very bad case—so bad that the doctor had very little hope for me one night. My heart was almost out of business. But no pneumonia developed and after ten days I crawled out of bed, collapsed, and had to be carried back to bed. I never, in all my life, was as utterly weak, nervous and depressed as that illness left me. I was three weeks before I felt anything like myself and to this day I feel the ill effects in heart and nerves.

I was just beginning to pick up when I got a telegram from Aunt Annie, saying that her only son George had died of pneumonia following influenza. This upset me terribly, for not only did I feel George's death but I realized what a forlorn plight those poor women, one old, one very delicate, with 6 small children, were in. In spite of my weakness I went at once to P. E. Island. My cousin Frede also went from Montreal and we waited on the sick (the whole family had the flu). One we could not save—little four-year-old Georgie died. The rest recovered. We disinfected the big house, and attended to all the business. Then I returned home the last of No-

vember and spent December in a feverish effort to finish my new book "Rainbow Valley" which should have
been done by the last of October. I finished it on New
Year's day. It will be published next August. It deals
with some adventures of Anne's *children* and their play-
mates.

Early in January I had to go to Boston where my lawsuit against the Page Co. finally came to a hearing. It has
been dragging on for three years, during which time
they have paid me no royalties. I had my very first experience in the witness box. I left it, feeling that I had
made all kinds of an ass of myself but when we left the
court my counsel said "You are such a good witness that
you ought to be in the witness stand all the time." Anyhow, I won my case and the Page Co. had to come across
with all the money they had been trying to cheat me out
of. I was glad, not only for our sake but for the sake of a
lot of authors who were being cheated by Page and who
were too timid or too poor to fight him in the courts. I
think it will make the Page Co. a little more inclined to
honesty as the best policy in future.

But I was not permitted to be glad long of my victory
over Page. I was already to start for home when I received a telegram saying that my cousin Mrs. McFarlane
(Frede Campbell)[4] was seriously ill with pneumonia following on flu. I left at once for Montreal and got there
Thursday morning. Frede died at sunrise Saturday
morning. I cannot tell you what this meant to me. I feel
as if half my life has been torn away. Frede and I have
been devoted friends all our lives. The tie between us
was of exceptional strength and depth. She was the most
wonderful woman I have ever known—so brilliant, so
witty, so companionable, so broad minded. For several
years she has been Demonstrator of Household Science
at Macdonald College near Montreal and head of the

4. She married Lieutenant N. Cameron MacFarlane on May 16,
   1917.

Women's Institute work for the province of Quebec. When the president of the college heard of her death he said, "Heavens, what a loss to the country," and that I think expressed the feeling of every one who ever knew her.

She was a "war bride," having married Lieut. N. C. MacFarlane before his departure for overseas. He is one of the 42 original "Princess Pats" who survived and is now coming home after four years of war, unscathed to find his wife dead of the plague the war brought in its train.

I came home after all was over, broken-hearted. The first unbearable agony has passed and now life just seems gray and bleak, with constant stabs of remembrance as every hour brings some reminder of what I have lost. I look forward to the spring with no thrill or pleasure. The war is over—but Frede has gone—whither? Where now is that unfailing humor, that flashing wit, that tender strength, that magnetic personality? The orthodox answers to that question do not satisfy me—bring me no comfort. Other friends say to me "I feel that Frede is near me." I who loved her best and was best loved by her, have no such feeling. The grave *hath* its sting, death *has* its victory—not perhaps over those who go, but for those and over those who remain. All the bereavements I have ever had, all put together, could not equal the agony of this loss. An old farmer down home who went to see Aunt Annie when he heard of Frede's death said to her "I feel sorrier for Mrs. Macdonald than for anyone else. Frede and her always seemed to me to be a *part of one another.*" He could not have expressed it better. For years before my marriage when Frede and I were both fighting the world alone we were constant chums and allies. She was with me when I was married. She was with me when Chester was born. She has spent all her holidays here. I was with her when she was married. I went to her four years ago when she

96

was thought to be dying of typhoid fever and the doctor said that it was my coming that gave her the necessary stimulus for the turn back to life. In all our great crises of life we have been together. But the gods do not like a friendship that supersedes them. God is a jealous god. And so—she went on and the gates closed between us.

And all this is why your letter has gone so long unanswered. I think you realize now that I spoke truly when I said no apology was needed.

We have had *no* winter here. There has been no snow, practically no cold weather. Cars and buggies have run right along. The like has never been known before— probably never will be again. It is all part of the abnormal conditions obtaining in the world.

The calendar you sent and the books also came safely to hand. I haven't had time to read the latter yet, as since coming home I have had to put every minute into catching up with all the work neglected since Xmas. But I hope soon to have a chance to read them and I promise myself much enjoyment. I have heard "Adventures in Contentment" spoken of very highly. I sent you one of Frank Stockton's books because he is my favorite American humorist and I suspected he would not be known to you. "Dudder Grange" is an old favorite of mine.

I enjoyed very much the topical verses you sent at different times. "King Coal" was especially good—or perhaps I thought so because of its aptness in our own coal famine. (We have had to burn wood all winter and it doesn't suit our furnace and *everything* is smoked up). Of the serious ones I liked "The Trooper" best. It's fine. Your songs are very beautiful too. You have improved wonderfully in the writing of these. They deserve success in the realm of music and I sincerely hope they may win it.

"St. Peter and the Soldier" *was* good. I think the *Gazette* publishes some really wonderful verses.

The Rev. Macdonald who won the Military Cross wasn't *my* Mr. Macdonald. I am—or suppose I should be—sorry to say.

Your poem "The Armageddon Steed" was capital. The idea was original and the treatment fine. I am compelled to notice all these more sketchily than I would like to, for this letter is already too long and my time is up. By the way this poem of yours reminds me to ask have you read the famous Spanish novel which is the best seller in America just now "The Four Horsemen of the Apocalypse." It is the best war novel I have read. Its restrained power is very remarkable.

You sent me three copies of the poem. If Frede were living I should at once have sent her one—as I sent everything, or a copy of everything that ever interested me. But she is gone. So I will paste one in my scrapbook and the others on the flyleaves of Chester and Stuart's books, that they may learn kindness for and appreciation of our dumb friends.

Yes, you were right as to my *not* being in Halifax when our correspondence began. It was Mr. Weber[5] with whom I began corresponding in Halifax. Since his marriage six or seven years ago our correspondence has been rather "seldom"—not that his wife objects at all— she seems to be a very charming little person—but because he seems to have little time for anything but his work. I suspect also he no longer suffers from the prairie loneliness which once drove him to seek the intellectual companionship of letters.

Mind *our* correspondence has lasted over fifteen years! Well, I hope you have found as much pleasure and inspiration in it as I have done and I also hope it will last as long as we live. *Afterwards,* if it is "ampler day divinelier lit" and not "starless night without," kindred intellects may have some way of communicating that is

5. Ephraim Weber (1871-1956) with whom she corresponds for some forty years.

better and more complete than clumsy pen and paper.
It may be only necessary to *think* our letters then.

There are many more things in your letter, your
verses, and my own notebook which I should like to
touch upon but space and time forbid it just now. I shall
mail this letter in two envelopes lest its bulk wear out
one. Mr. Macdonald sends kind remembrances.

With all good wishes.

Yours sincerely,
L. M. Macdonald

The Manse
Leaskdale, Ont.

Aug. 23, 1920

Dear Mr. MacMillan:

It's considerably over the year this time, isn't it? That is
worse rather than better. But truly it has been my misfortune not my fault. This past year and a half has been
one of trial and anxiety for me. A year ago last May Mr.
Macdonald took suddenly very ill. The doctor here
called it nervous prostration but could discover no
cause. He advised rest and change. So Mr. M. went
down to his sister's in Boston. He had been there only a
couple of weeks when he became so violently ill that
they wired me to come at once. I left my children here
with my maid and went at once, expecting not to find
my husband alive. But he was somewhat better when I
arrived. The specialist had discovered the cause of his
trouble. For some reason—probably a cold setting in
them—his kidneys had ceased to function properly with
the result that his whole system was being poisoned, the
nerves and the heart especially being affected, the result
being terrible headaches, insomnia and collapses. As
soon as proper treatment was begun he began to re-

cover but it was the middle of August before he could travel. Then we came home.

.   .   .

When I last wrote you I was in the bitterness of recent bereavement—and yet am. But time has brought a certain healing, the sharp flame of agony has burned itself out and the gray dust of ashes is over my world. Yet I miss my friend as much as I did the month after she died—nay, even more I think, for then the very anguish of my grief seemed to *fill life* and now that it has gone I realize the emptiness. I wonder if it will ever by any easier to live without her. I do not think that since Frede died there has been *one* waking hour in which I have not thought of her, or one day in which there has not been, at some moment or other a pang of remembrance that pierced soul and spirit. In one of the *Westminster Gazettes* you sent me many months ago, a prize was offered for the best verse whose first line should be,

"*If I should live your epitaph to write.*"

There were two verses in that contest which clung to my memory and come into my mind whenever I think of Frede, especially the first one:—

"*If I should live your epitaph to write,*
Naught would I say but 'I, too died that night.' "

Something of *me* died with Frede and can never live again.

The other verse appeals to me also, with a little note of comfort in it which I cannot find in many things:—

"*If I should live your epitaph to write*
I'd pen no more than this: 'True friend, good night,
And when I too have slept if first you wake
Bid me, good-morrow for our old love's sake.' "

Yes, I agree with you that it is *not* desirable to think that our friends who have died, *are* near us *all* the time. Indeed, the thought would be a horrible one. But if we

The Macneill
homestead in
Cavendish (above)
COURTESY: DR. STUART
MACDONALD

L. M. Montgomery
at the time the
correspondence
begins (left)
COURTESY: RUTH CAMPBELL

The Reverend Ewen Macdonald, Presbyterian minister in Cavendish (above) COURTESY DR. STUART MACDONALD

L. M. Montgomery in a dress from her trousseau (right) COURTESY RUTH CAMPBELL

Campbell home at Park Corner where L. M. Montgomery was married in 1911 (below) COURTESY DR. STUART MACDONALD

George Boyd MacMillan (above) COURTESY: MOLLIE GILLEN

L. M. Montgomery in her going-away outfit (left) COURTESY: MRS. MARGARET WHITEHEAD

Postcard written during the honeymoon to Emily Montgomery (below) COURTESY: RUTH CAMPBELL

The Leaskdale Manse COURTESY: DR. STUART MACDONALD

Stuart COURTESY: RUTH CAMPBELL

Chester

COURTESY: RUTH CAMPBELL

Fredericka Campbell

COURTESY: RUTH CAMPBELL

The Macdonald family (left to right: Ewen, Chester, Stuart, a friend, L. M. Montgomery)

Left: "The little picture of myself among the P. E. Island daisies is really the best *likeness* of me I've ever had taken." (August 26, 1924). She sent this picture as a Christmas card in 1924.

at. you. Daff!

Daffy, one of her favourite cats COURTESY: RUTH CAMPBELL

Ernest and Myrtle Webb's home purchased by Parks Canada and now called "Green Gables"

COURTESY: DR. STUART MACDONALD

Norval Manse (above)

COURTESY: ANITA WEBB

L. M. Montgomery
in the 1930s (left)

COURTESY: RUTH CAMPBELL

The Reverend Ewen Macdonald and Mrs. Macdonald on their retirement from Norval COURTESY: RUTH CAMPBELL

"Journey's End" COURTESY: DR. STUART MACDONALD

could only *feel* them near when we *need* them—when we desire them to be near—what a comfort it would be!

In connection with this I am going to tell you something which I have told few. It is not a thing that should be told to many. There is a ridiculous aspect of it, I know; yet it has never seemed ridiculous to me. One day over a year ago Chester's eye was injured. He came home from school with the eye swelled shut and bleeding from an accident in school when a playmate had thrown a sharp stick at him. Eventually, I may say right here, the injury proved to be trifling and transitory but at the time we did not know what it was and the doctor feared that the ball might have been punctured. It was necessary to give C. chloroform in order to examine the eye. Chester had never been given chloroform and I could not tell how it would affect him. Reason told me that he would probably be all right but that did not prevent my nerves from going to pieces when the moment arrived. I made Mr. Mcd. go up with the doctor. Once I could have gone but since my attack of "flu" I have *no* nerve. I could not go. Instead, I shut myself in the parlor and sat down with clenched hands and with teeth on the rug to *wait.*

"Oh, if only Frede were with me now," I moaned. Then the thought came suddenly "Perhaps she is. If human personality truly survives death I *know* that Frede would be with me in any crisis. But I want to *know* it. Is there no way in which I can *know?*"

I felt at that moment that I *must* know it if it were so. I had no *feeling* that she was near, such as I have heard others speak of.

My old gray cat "Daffy" had come in and was sitting gravely by the door. Frede had always made a great pet of him and had always insisted that he understood every word she said to him—as indeed, he certainly appeared to do in more than one uncanny instance. Suddenly I remembered reading that animals are aware of presences which human beings cannot sense. Perhaps it was also true that these presences had some influence over animals. *If Frede were with me could she make our old pet and comrade do something which would prove her presence to me!*

I reflected for a moment. I would ask for some unlikely thing—something that Daff had never done in his life.

"Frede," I said in a tense whisper "if you are here *make Daff come over to me and kiss me.*"

Daff *never* offered any caresses or sought or enjoyed petting. Yet it is the literal truth, that, as soon as the words left my lips the cat walked gravely across the room to me, lifted her forepaws and placed them on my shoulders, and touched my cheek with his mouth. Moreover, he did it twice.

Written out, this thing looks ridiculous. Why do such experiences always seem ridiculous when written or told? Perhaps because they should *not* be written or told—only lived. There was nothing that seemed ridiculous at the time. Instead, I felt sure that Frede *was* there with me and had made her old furry comrade the medium of her message. The conviction brought comfort and strength and calmness. Since then, the conviction has grown dim and scepticism has crept in. But it seemed very strange and real at the time; and certainly Daff did there what he never did before or since.

And speaking of poor Daff—we had a family tragedy here just two weeks ago. We found him dying one morning. Thought first that he had been poisoned but discovered that he had been shot—by whom or how we do not know. It was likely accidental as there is no one hereabouts who would have knowingly shot him. I can't tell you how much I miss him. I had him for over fourteen years; he was not a cat—he was a *person*. He was my last living link with the old life and he had been my constant companion for the most vivid and intense years of my life. His intelligence was uncanny and in spite of his age his eye was not dim nor his vivacity abated. I believe he would have lived several years yet for there was no sign of age about him except that he was not quite so agile at jumping as he used to be or quite so fond of a fight. I feel as if I never could bear to have another cat—Daff has spoiled me for any other. He was the handsomest cat I ever saw—silver gray with black markings. He was sent up to me from the Island by express after I came back from my wedding tour and everybody in the congregation took an interest in him. We buried him in a corner of the lawn, but the house and grounds seem to be haunted by him, for he had so many favorite nooks according to season or time of day. I miss him most when I come home at night after being out for the evening. It was his invariable habit to meet me at the gate and frisk ahead of me up the walk. Well, I'm going to stop right here and now, for if I keep on I shall feel too badly to write anymore. Dear old Daff was a friend and comrade and deserves to be mourned and remembered. "He was a cat—take him for all in all, I shall not look upon his like again."

．　　．　　．

I finished my new book[1] yesterday and sent it off to the typewriter with a sigh of relief. Its title is yet undecided but it is more of a "girl's story" than my previous two, dealing with the life of a Canadian girl during the years of the war. It is positively the last of the *Anne* series. I have gone completely "stale" on Anne and *must* get a new heroine. Six books are enough to write about any one girl. I am sick of her and I wonder the public isn't, too. Yet they don't seem to be. I had an amusing letter recently from a young girl asking if "Anne" hadn't "kept a diary" and if so wouldn't I publish it! And I had a pathetic letter from a lady, telling me that her father, a retired army officer of 85 loved the Anne books so and

1. *Rilla of Ingleside.*

was worrying lest he would not live until the next one came out. This is touching. But I must try to create another heroine who will enter into Anne's legacy of love.

Now, my very good friend, I shall close this rambling epistle, which is a sort of hotch-potch of everything I think. Oh, I forgot to say that the little poem you sent "Trees" has long been beloved by me. I have it in my book of gems. The author, as I suppose you know, was killed "somewhere in France."

Yours fraternally.
L. M. Macdonald

P.S. I enjoyed your Xmas books richly. "The Friendly Road" is a dear thing. What *did* people do before printing was invented? No wonder they burned each other to enliven life!

The Manse
Leaskdale, Ont.

September 14, 1922

Dear Mr. MacMillan:

. . .

I have just re-read your letter to refresh my memory of it and *taste* it again. Somehow, to me, letters are much like *soup,* in that they always seem to be improved in flavor when "warmed over." They must ripen and grow mellow in the meantime. I always get more enjoyment out of the second reading of a letter or a book than out of the first. I've had a real good time re-reading your letter to-night; but the dickens of it is that it has taken quite a while and now it is bed time and I can't write any more of this only begun letter to-night. I dare not sit up later for I must rise be-times to get the boys' breakfast, prepare their lunches, and start them off to school, having first duly put them through the "mother's cate-chism"—viz!—

1. Have you washed your face, neck and ears?
2. Have you brushed your hair?
3. Have you brushed your teeth?
4. Have you cleaned your fingernails?
5. Have you a clean handkerchief?
6. Have you got on both garters?
7. Are you sure there are no holes in your stockings?
8. Have you got your pencils and scribblers?

So I must get my forty winks before then and leave the rest of this till "next stint." Good-night!

September 24th

. . .

By the law of *dis*-association of ideas—how do you like "free verse"? I loathe it. I saw a delightful definition of it the other day—"shredded prose"—although the full delight of the definition will be lost upon you if you are not familiar with the breakfast cereal known as "shredded wheat." *Vers libre* aggravates me beyond my powers of expression.

> *"I feel*
> *Very much*
> *Like taking*
> *Its unholy perpetrators*
> *By the hair*
> *Of their heads,*
> *(If they have any hair)*
> *And dragging them around*
> *The yard*
> *A few times*
> *And then cutting them*
> *Into small, irregular pieces*
> *And burying them*
> *In the depths of the blue sea.*
> *They are without form*

And void,
Or at least
The stuff they produce
Is.
They are too lazy
To hunt up rhymes
And that
is all
That is the matter with them."
I feel better.

Mr. Macdonald has been better this summer than anytime since 1918. I am hoping that the improvement in his health will continue. Last year he was not very well by times.

.   .   .

We have been enjoying our car muchly this summer. We have a new one—a Grey Dort. We call her Lady Jane Grey Dort. We were in a terrible motor accident a year ago last spring—a head-on collision with another car which was going at a terrific rate of speed and never turned off the road. The cars were all smashed up. How we escaped with our lives I don't know. Nobody was much injured but I had a terrible shock and was weeks getting over it. We had the children with us too. Here is a curious thing. After the collision I was perfectly calm and unconcerned. The only thing I was worried about was a *borrowed hymn book* which I had in my hand just before the collision—we were coming home from church—and which had disappeared. How could I account for it to the owner? This mood continued for half an hour. Then all at once I began to cry and went to pieces!

I suppose I was mentally stunned.

Last summer we motored all the way to P. E. Island and back—almost 3000 miles. A wonderful trip in many ways but pretty fatiguing, especially with children. The first day we reached Kingston. Next morning crossed the St. Lawrence to Watertown N.Y. and motored all day reaching the Berkshire Mts. at night. Next day we climbed the Berkshire range and "coasted" for twenty miles down "Jacob's Ladder"—a wonderful experience. We reached Springfield Mass. that night and next day reached Boston where we stayed until Sunday noon. We "picknicked" along the road and had jolly little meals. Sunday afternoon we motored to Portland along the New England coast—a delightful road with the Atlantic waves rolling in in great gray misty breakers. We motored for two days through the great pine woods of Maine, crossed New Brunswick and so over to the Island. We spent a delightful two weeks there then came home by a different route across Maine and Vermont through the Green Mts.

By the way, I had a luncheon the other day with Mrs. Pankhurst of suffragette fame—the redoubtable Emmeline in the flesh. As I looked at her I could not see the smasher of London windows and the hunger striker forcibly fed in Holloway jail. She had a sweet tired gentle face—looked like some Presbyterian elder's wife in a country village who had had nothing more strenuous in her life than running the local Ladies Aid and putting up with the elder.

I had an interesting trip to Cleveland, Ohio, last fall, to speak to a Woman's Club there. One evening we dined at a "cabaret," listened to "jazz" music and watched the modern dances concerning which there are such skeils of wrath in the journals of the period. I hardly wondered. I have always liked dancing—the dancing of my girlhood—but truth to tell, some of the couples I saw there (*not* all—many really danced unobjectionably) reminded me of Byron's biting line, "Nor leave much mystery for the nuptial night." But then Byron wrote that of the old waltz, which now is considered a very dignified, graceful dance. So perhaps our descendants will tell their children that the horrible dances in vogue are terrible—"so different from the becoming fox trots and bunny hops of 1920!"

. . . .

Last February I finished my new book "Emily of New Moon." I had more pleasure in writing it than in any book since *Green Gables*, because I had a new subject I suppose. It will not be out till 1923. I hope you will like the dedication.

. . .

We spent two weeks in Muskoka this summer. It is the famous summer resort of Canada and is about 85 miles from here. It is more like fairyland than any place I ever saw—not even excepting the *Lake District* of England—a dream of lakes and maple woods and islands and lovely summer cottages.

Have you ever had this experience? You are somewhere on a vacation. You have many pleasant hours—picnics, drives, sails, games. Yet when you come to the end the thing that stands out most vividly in memory as the dearest pleasantest time of all was none of these, but something that nobody else would have supposed was very wonderful at all. This happened to me at Muskoka.

One evening I sat all alone for two hours on the verandah of our boarding house (I enclose a picture of it by the way and the *white dot* on the verandah just above the steps is *me*. For I have a second claim to fame. I'm on a picture postal, of which this picture is a magazine reproduction!) Well, I sat there alone. Everybody else was away on a motor launch trip. I could not go because I had hurt my foot. When the others came back they were most sympathetic and pitied me for missing a lovely time. I smiled to myself—for I had had a *glorious time* and the fragrance of it has lingered in memory ever since as the *supreme hour* of my holiday.

The river before the house was silver under the moon. The lights of the cottages twinkled along the woods on the opposite bank. Bonfires blazed here and there with all the old allure of campfires, music and laughter drifted up to me from the innumerable canoes and launches on the water. The big pines behind the house sighed and murmured. Thought seemed unusually quick with me—imagination unusually vivid. I was in a mood I recognized at once as the perfect one for dreaming. So I dreamed. I picked out an island that suited me (the Muskoka lakes and rivers are dotted with islands). I built thereon a summer cottage and furnished it deluxe. I set up a boat house and a motor launch. I peopled it with summer guests—all kindred spirits. Dear old Aunt Annie—my cousin Frede who died in 1919 but who lived again in my dream—my cousin Bertie McIntyre[1] whom I have not seen for six years, and *you*. There you all were, as our "house party" guests. We spent a whole idyllic summer there. I lived it out in every detail. We swam and sailed and fished and dived and sat out summer sunsets on moonlit porches (well screened from Muskoka mosquitoes) and always we *talked*—the soul-satisfying talk of congenial souls. Sometimes we varied it by going out to dinners and *dances* (in my dream Ewan was *not* a minister!) at the houses on neighboring islands, enjoying them tremendously but always glad to skim back home over the moonlit wonder channels to our own island. I dreamed it all out to the end of September. Then one night a storm came up. You and Ewan and the boys had gone to

---

1. Beatrice A. McIntyre, to whom L.M. dedicated *Kilmeny of the Orchard*.

the mainland in the motor launch. We women waited for your return through the wild night while the hurricane tore through the channels and the waves dashed over rocks to our very doors. Frede struggled down to the pier and held out a lantern. You and Ewan saw it and found your way to land, drenched and cold but safe. And we joyfully shut our door on the storm and all sat down to a hot supper before the blazing fire in our living room. I pictured out every dish in that supper. And we laughed and talked and were happy, surrounded by the blackness of the storm. But we knew that our summer was over. The next day Bertie must go back to Vancouver, Frede to Macdonald College, you to Scotland, Ewan and I home.

How silly and babyish it all seems written out. And how vital and delightful it was in my dream. And how it remains in my memory as distinct as any of the days we really lived there. Then the others came home and I came back to "real life." There was no fairyland—Frede slept dreamlessly in her grave by a far-off ocean. Yet not two minutes before she had been laughing at me across my supper table in the firelight and I had heard the very cadences of her voice as she described her wild buffet through the storm to the boat-house and her joy when she heard Ewan's hail out of the darkness! And *you* had been flirting with Bertie!

Yes, you will say "She's quite crazy, poor thing!"

But it was a charming madness.

It is nearly twelve o'clock. I'm going to bed. I enclose some snaps of our Muskoka sojourn—but my fairy Island isn't among them, alas. You will find their significance written on the back.

This sheet is positively just to say good-bye on. If you answer this letter in *less* than six months I swear I'll do the same—and in my next "dreaming" I'll marry you to

Bertie (who is a duck) and you'll live happily every after.

Yours most sincerely,
L. M. Montgomery Macdonald

P.S.   I *have* finished the letter and I *haven't* busted.

P.S. No. 2   After all I forgot to tell you something that happened in a Toronto store the other day—an odd little coincidence. I thought at the time "I mustn't forget to tell Mr. McMillan that when I write him." It will serve as an admirable commentary on Kipling's famous couplet

> *"The colonel's lady and Judy O'Grady*
> *Are sisters under their skins."*

As I halted at a counter in the millinery dept. I overheard a snatch of conversation between two women who were standing near—evidently women of culture and wealth. "My dear, she has a *perfectly lovely* husband."

Then I went down to the basement. In the elevator were two other women plainly of a very inferior grade of society and they too, seemed to be discussing a mutual friend and as I stepped out of the elevator I heard one say "Gosh, but she's got a *swell man.*"

PART II

The Manse
Leaskdale, Ont.

September 3/24

Dear Mr. MacMillan:

I begin number two, feeling a bit sleepy. We were down to Uxbridge last night and stayed rather late listening in on a friend's radio. It was all very wonderful—but do you know I found it a little *depressing*. Is it because I'm getting on in life that all these wonderful inventions and discoveries, treading on each other's heels, give me a sense of *weariness* and a longing to go back to the slower years of old? Doubtless that *has* something to do with it. But I really do think we are rushing on rather fast. It keeps humanity on tiptoe. But I think this will go on for two or three hundred years more—I mean the flood of great discoveries and inventions. Then probably *Zeit Geist* will get tired and take a rest for a few centuries and allow humanity to rest with him. But those of us living now have to speed on with him willy-nilly.

In a few generations *letters* will be obsolete. Everyone will *talk* to absent friends the world over by *radio*. It will be nice; but something will be lost with letters. The world can't eat its cake and have it too. And none of these things really "save time." They only fill it more breathlessly full. That may be all right for the young. But I look back to the old '90's with the feeling that they were a nice unhurried leisurely time.

．　　．　　．

Did I ever tell you that, in the winter of 1923 the Royal Society of Arts of Great Britain selected me a "Fellow"

112

of the Society? So I have the right if I wish to write F.R.S.A. after my name! I suppose it is quite a compliment. I was the first Canadian woman to be so honored, though some Canadian men are members. It was rather funny and not a little disgusting to note the jealousy it aroused among certain Canadian writers who seemed to think the honor should have been bestowed elsewhere!

Well, I was a wee bit pleased with it. But after all it didn't give me half as much pleasure as I felt when my small lad Stuart said gravely to me the other day, "I hope if I am ever born again *you* will be born again as my mother." Now, wasn't *that* real nice?

Stuart is always making us laugh. The other night he was sitting, looking very grave, suddenly he drew a long sigh and said, "Oh, mother I wish I were grown-up and married and *had it over with.*"

It was very funny and yet I sighed a little behind my laughter. Stuart has evidently inherited my tendency to cross bridges before he comes to them. It means a lot of unnecessary worry through life. And yet—perhaps it is the foresight and preparation induced by the worry that makes the bridge safe!

Later on in the evening Stuart pursued the same line of investigation.

"Mother when I get married will I have to give her a ring?"

"Yes," I said.

"And will I have to kiss her?"

"It is not compulsory," I said gravely. "You need not kiss her unless you want to."

"I am glad of that," said Stuart in a relieved tone, "because I don't want to kiss any girl except my mother."

I think it is highly probable that *this* is a bridge which Stuart will find very easy to cross!!!

I had a rare and real pleasure to-night. We went to call on one of our families and after I had done my duty for awhile talking to a woman who was, in Milton's expressive phrase "stupidly good" I decided to run over to the next farm and call on a widow there. I took a short cut through the orchard and across two fields green with clover aftermath, and for fifteen minutes I was *alone* with Nature again as I have very rarely been of late years. It was unbelievably lovely. Solitude was with me like a sweet-lipped friend. A fresh world of fairy-blue hills and spacious fields was all about me. Over me was a violet sky with a red Mars in the south. I was knee-deep in clover and fragrant grasses. I felt "an April-hearted thing" once more—young, happy, care-free. My soul brimmed over. Oh, that it should be of such short duration. For soon I had left my fairyland behind me and was listening to the rather weird conversation of an old lady whose mind is not quite rational. I had to listen to a minute account of the death and illness of her husband—who was a miserly old curmudgeon of no use to God or man. He never had a thought above the dollar sign in his life and would have sold his soul if he had one—for thirty pieces of silver any day. But the old lady gave me in full her reasons for believing that in spite of all "his name was written in the Lamb's Book of Life." There was something both pathetic and tragic in her efforts to convince me—and herself—that it was so. She was afraid in her secret heart that her husband had gone to hell—as logically he should have if the convictions she has held all her life were true—and she was also afraid that public opinion would think he had, which was a humiliating thing. So the minister's wife must know how she had read the Bible to him and how he had said "Yes, ma," when she told him that these were the words of eternal life. No, I didn't laugh, even to myself. I didn't feel at all like laughing. I repeat that I found it pathetic and tragic, and I wondered what the God with whom I had been in close communion half an hour before on that windy green hill of clover would think of it all. Would he not have said, "Ye are all my children, blind, helpless, stumbling, mistaken, torturing yourselves with the creeds and dogmas of your own invention. In death I open a door and give you rest."

In the summer of 1923 I spent a beautiful six weeks down on P. E. Island. It was one of those ideal vacations that so rarely come—when everything goes according to your plans and is wholly satisfying. My first week was spent with an old college chum in her summer bungalow on the south side, built just where the North River empties into Hillsborough bay. It was situated between two range lights that burned enchantingly through the twilights, pearl white against the ethereal skies. Down the harbor there were more rangelights and far out, seemingly in mid-harbor, shone the far away lighthouse on Point Prim—a beacon in "fairylands forlorn."

Next to us was a vacant lot full of daisies—the one where was taken the snap I sent you. It was a place of haunted loveliness in the twilights—and over the river were daisied fields as white as snow. I always go back to a realization of the Island's beauty with a certain amazement. I have always forgotten that it is really *so* lovely. There is nothing like it in smug opulent Ontario. I used to slip down to the shore in the late dusk, feeling how beautiful it was to be alone with the night again, with the stars all in their right places over me, and gaze on water and field and hill with eyes that would devour them.

Then I went up to Cavendish. Delight again. Some old gladness always waits there for me and leaps into my heart as soon as I return. The evenings there were wonderful. A pale silver moon shone in the sky. The roads were of that brilliant red peculiar to P. E. Island roads on a dewy evening after sunset. There were exquisite views of pond and dunes and harbor all bathed in opal dust. A certain part of my soul long starved mounted up on wings as of eagles. I was at home—heart and soul and mind I was at home. My years of exile had vanished. I had never been away.

115

We spent many afternoons on the sandshore. There's nothing in all the world like that shore. But one poetry has vanished from the gulf forever. It is never now dotted with hundreds of white sails. The fishermen now have motor boats which chug-chug out in the morning and chug-chug back at night and are not on speaking terms with romance.

From Cavendish I went to Park Corner to see Aunt Annie. Park Corner is, as you may remember, where I was married and the home of my dear friend Frede, who died. There was sorrow mingled with the pleasure here. I missed Frede so much. Here was the mirror that had reflected her face. But where was she? Where was the savor and vivacity of her speech?

But Aunt Annie was so glad to have me that her gladness surrounded me with a warm pleasant feeling. Old Park Corner was beautiful still—the birches down the lane were as white and stately as of yore.

One day I went to Bedeque to speak to a camp of C.G.I.T.'s (Canadian Girls in Training). The camp was in a lovely spot and at first I felt as if I envied those girls. But on consideration I concluded I did not. I never liked a crowd; and to live in the woods with several overseers to watch every step wouldn't please me at all. To be there alone with one kindred spirit—that would be the right sort of camping. To bask on the clover in the sunshine—bathe in the flaming river at sunset—loaf on the bracken in the woods—sit in twilight by a campfire—tell the stars at midnight over the dark woods—and feel always near at hand, within touch or call, the comrade who understood.

I was impressed by one thing—the plainness to the point of homeliness of the C.G.I.T.'s. They seemed bright and jolly but with one exception there was of beauty little and of charm not a trace. That exception was a little slip of a girl with brown hair, a delicious complexion and a fillet of June bell vine around her head

116

that gave her the look of a young oread or spruce-wood nymph. She was the only one I could conceive a man falling in love romantically with. I think the sporting flapper of today has lost something. The girls of my day, as I recall them, had more of lure and mystery.

I had a great many buggy drives at Park Corner and enjoyed them so much. The auto is all right for long journeys, bad weather or a crowd. But for sheer, simple pleasure I would choose a horse and buggy every time. I enjoyed every minute of those drives, poking along and finding at every turn or curve one of the arch, provocative elusive beauties of a P.E.I. landscape. Then we would drive home in the gray twilight. There is one of the most wonderful views on the Island from a certain hill back of Park Corner and the melancholy loveliness of the night wind off the sea sent an almost physical pang through me.

I felt very badly at leaving Park Corner. Aunt Annie was 75 and I had a miserable foreboding that she would not be there when I came again—a foreboding all too completely fulfilled.

And now having finished telling you about my 1923 vacation I'll close this part and send it off. Part III will follow in due time, if ye faint not.

Yours suspensively
L. M. Macdonald

PART III

Last fall was a very busy one—we had so many church entertainments and celebrations. It seemed that we were no sooner over one than we were engulfed in the preparations for another. I took one day off and we motored into Toronto to see and hear Lloyd George in

Massey Hall. I had not expected to get tickets but Mr. McClelland my publisher pulled wires and got them for us. There were 3000 tickets and 180,000 applications!

We saw and heard "the little Welshman"—I don't think he is as tall as I am "from the neck down." He was very hoarse and we could not hear all his speech. What we could hear was not so very wonderful. But it was the man himself—the man of the Great War. I think Lloyd George is and always will be considered one of the most intriguing characters in history. He is essentially a fighter. He is lost without something to fight. He did more than any one man or score of men to win the war. But I think his day is done. He is not a constructive statesman, such as is sorely needed now. But he *had* his day—and did his work—and it was for this that we all sprang to our feet as he came out on the platform and shouted and hurrahed and clapped and stamped and *cried*—and would have flung ourselves down and let him walk over us if he had wanted to.

I finished my second Emily book in February—but of course it won't be out till next year. By dint of writing 3 hours per diem as instead of only two as formerly I am beginning to get nicely ahead with my work and losing that hateful feeling of breathlessness I have had for years. Of course Emily II (haven't a title for it yet) isn't half as good as Emily of New Moon. The second volume of a series, especially if it deals with a very young girl, is the hardest for me to. write—because the public and publisher won't allow me to write of a young girl as she really is. One can write of children as they are; so my books about children are always good; but when you come to write of the "miss" you have to depict a sweet insipid young thing—really a child grown older—to whom the basic realities of life and reactions to them are quite unknown. *Love* must scarcely be hinted at—yet young girls often have some very vivid love affairs. A girl of *Emily's* type certainly would. But the public—

118

One of the Vanderbilts once said "Damn the public."
I'm just saying what one of the Vanderbilts said. I'm not saying it myself.

I can't afford to damn the public. I must cater to it for awhile yet.

.   .   .

On the 19th of June dear Aunt Annie died after an illness of several weeks which were weeks of suspense and misery to me. Just before her death I had a very remarkable psychic experience. Perhaps I shall tell you about it sometime. I can't write of it just now.

I went down to Park Corner to attend her funeral. There were some terrible moments when I reached Park Corner and no Aunt Annie came to meet me—for the first time no Aunt Annie. I went in to look for the last time on that kind beloved face which had always looked upon me with a maternal smile.

Aunt Annie lying in her casket in that softly lighted old parlor was the most beautiful thing I ever saw. She looked like a young girl. Her dark hair in which there was hardly a thread of gray was waved over her forehead. There was not a wrinkle on the peaceful face and she wore a little dress of white silk.

I do not remember Aunt Annie young. As far back as I can remember she was or seemed elderly, and always wore dark sober dresses. Now I saw her as a girl. And yet it is not as that marble white bride of death that I shall remember Aunt Annie. No, I shall think of her as the old woman in a gingham apron coming out of her pantry and feeding her chickens. Aunt Annie was always *feeding* something—human beings or animals. She was always *giving*. She had had much sorrow in her life and many disappointments but nothing had ever broken her spirit or embittered her heart. Death gave her back her old beauty and—perhaps—her old happiness. At least peace and rest.

On July 25th my cousin and dear old pal of childhood, Bertie McIntyre, came from Vancouver to visit me and she and I and Ewan took a motor trip to Kentucky to see the Mammoth Cave. We left here the morning of Monday July 28 and arrived back Thursday evening Aug 7, after a very delightful trip of 1817 miles, with not one drop of rain or one bit of car trouble. This was such good luck as to be positively uncanny. The first day we went from Leaskdale to Sarnia—a good lap. Next morning we crossed to the U.S. and went down through Michigan crossing into Indiana in the evening. Our objective was Fort Wayne but darkness overtook us at *Hicksville* and at Hicksville we stayed.

I don't know what Hicksville is like. I did not see much of it. It *may* have every virtue. In it may live people, pure of soul, lofty of aspiration. Mute, inglorious Miltons may throng its streets; gems of purest ray serene may sparkle in its social galaxy. But to me Hicksville Ind. will always connote—bedbugs!

No, no, let me be just—exact. Let me not exaggerate. *One* bedbug.

Bertie and I discovered him in our room, peacefully traversing a pillow. Naturally we went mad. We fell upon that bed and tore it to pieces. I flew to Ewan's room and dragged everything off his and the boys beds. But we found no more. Evidently that bug believed that he travels the fastest who travels alone and had formed no family ties. Nevertheless B. and I slept on the floor that night.

We reached Warsaw, Ind. at noon Wednesday where Mr. Macdonald's brother Dr. Angus Macdonald lives. We had dinner with him and his wife and stayed there until three, then "hit the pike again."

We made Indianapolis that night (get a map of the U.S. and follow our course). The scenery down through Indiana was monotonous. Any one place was pretty enough but it was all fatally the same mile after mile of fertile farmlands and little villages with hanging baskets.

But we made our own fun and enjoyed the road until about four or five o'clock. Then invariably every evening the testing time came. We suddenly became aware that we were tired, hungry and disgruntled. At least I always felt so and I have no doubt Bertie and Ewan felt the same. I can't be quite sure for none of us ever failed to emerge victoriously from the test. No one ever exploded. So I think we did remarkably well for if things got on their nerves about that time as they did on mine we must have been three combustible creatures under our exterior calmness and courtesy. At such times I wished I had never left home and vowed that I would *never* start on a long trip again. What fools people were to go whirling across the continent in this crazy fashion, getting dusty and dirty—oh, how dirty!—and scandalously tired. The ceaseless questions of the boys drove me frantic. Yes, a long auto trip in the heat of summer is as good a test as I know. People who can pass it successfully need not be afraid of any other.

Then we would get to our hotel, get bathed and dressed and sit down to a good meal. Presto change! Everything was all right. A motor trip through strange lands was a delightful thing, Bertie was a dear, witty companionable creature, the boys regular little bricks of travellers.

Thursday—what a day that was! All went well to Louisville and for some miles beyond. The prairies were behind us and the Kentucky hills around us. The scenery was beautiful and the roads fair. *And* they were of our own bright Island red. This amazed me. I had never heard that Kentucky had red roads. But it has. And I shall never forget them.

Beyond Camp Knox the Dixie Highway was closed, being under construction. We had to make two detours—forty five miles in all. I never was on anything in my life like that detour. The mountain road in Maine, where our Gray Dort broke down on our trip east in

121

1921, was terrible. But it was a boulevard compared to that awful Kentucky detour of hills and sloughs, bumps and rocks. Darkness overtook us on it. It seemed literally endless. What if our car broke down as break down it *must* on such a road. No car could get through it alive. And what would we do? We were twenty miles from any kind of help.

Dodgie did get through. Not a thing happened to her or us.

Some things are foreordained—and other things are just darn sheer luck.

The next day at the Cave we heard lurid tales of what had happened to cars on that road. One party of tourists were out all night on it and had to be towed back to Louisville the next day. And the towing car broke down and *both* had to be towed. One man at the Cave, being asked if he were a tourist replied grumpily, "No, I'm a *de*tourist."

. . .

Yours indefinitely
L. M. Macdonald

The Norval Letters

(letters from 1926 to 1935)

The first letter to MacMillan from Norval, Ontario, explains that the Macdonalds have left Leaskdale because of the Church Union controversy. Adjustment to the new life in Norval is complicated by a number of worries.

The first Norval letter introduces the lawsuit with the Page Company over Further Chronicles of Avonlea, *that "illegitimate offspring" she never acknowledges (she gives the full story in February 10, 1929). In letter after letter she refers to Ewen's continuing poor health; he eventually has a complete physical breakdown.*

The tone of the letters during the Norval years is nostalgic. She talks about growing old and frequently reminisces about her youth. She remarks to MacMillan in the last letter from Norval: "It seems somehow pleasant to revisit the past and so forget the present."

Despite the problems of "the present," she publishes six novels while in Norval: The Blue Castle *(1926),* Emily's Quest *(1927),* Magic for Marigold *(1929),* A Tangled Web *(1931),* Pat of Silver Bush *(1933), and* Mistress Pat *(1935).*

Once again, the letters describing her holidays on the Island are highlights of the correspondence.

The Manse
<u>Norval</u>, Ont.

Sunday
Aug. 29/26

Dear Mr. MacMillan:

It still seems strange to write "Norval" at the head of my letters instead of "Leaskdale," especially when beginning a letter to anyone to whom I have not yet written since our "flitting." But of said flitting will I not write until I come to it in its own place, in the chronicle of existence since my last letter to you in October 1924. Nearly two years. What a terrible gap. I agree *in toto* with your suggestion that we try to get back to the old basis of shorter and more frequent letters. Things "grow cold" and lose their flavor when they are kept so long. An item that seemed vital at the time and might have interested one's correspondent seems after a few months too trivial and insignificant to consume paper and time for, or is elbowed out of the field of consciousness by newer or seemingly bigger things. So I will begin to-day to answer the grist of your letters labelled "part I" and so on, send my answer in one packet and so wipe out my epistolary debts to youward, that we may start afresh and neither of us run so deeply in debt again.

.　　.　　.

Further Chronicles of Avonlea!!! So you have discovered the dark and deadly secret of my past! That illegitimate offspring which I have never acknowledged! That sole stain on an otherwise spotless career!

Joking apart, I was surprised to learn that you didn't know about that book. I knew I hadn't sent you a copy— catch me!—but I did think I had at least mentioned it. I suppose I did not. The whole matter has always been so

124

bitter to me that I hated to mention it to anyone. I have always meant to tell you the whole story *when it should be completed. Six years ago* I brought suit against Page over his publication of that book. *That suit is not yet concluded* though I believe another year will see the end of it. I thought I *had* mentioned the book itself to you but I knew I had said nothing about the lawsuit, because I was waiting until it was finished. It would take a book to tell it fully. You can never realize Mr. MacMillan the worry, misery, *sus*pense and *ex*pense with which this wretched litigation has filled my life for the past six years. I have won again and again and they have appealed again and again even carrying it to the Supreme Court of the U.S. They had no right to give the book to Harrap because I got an injunction against its publication two years ago. However, I will say no more about it now. When the suit is finally wound up I will write a special letter telling you the whole weird tale and I'll send you a copy of the book as well. It may be valuable as a "curiosity" in a generation or so, when my "diary" is published with a full account of the whole curious transaction. So hang on to it when you get it!!! And remind me if I forget.

·　·　·

October 13th

After supper this evening Stuart and I raked fallen leaves and had a bonfire of them. While they were burning we prowled about star hunting. We re-found Aquarius, Fomalhaut, Aquila, Corona, the Pleiades and the Hyades. I recalled the days of fifteen or sixteen years ago when I roamed over the Cavendish hills and fields in spring and summer and autumn twilights star-hunting. This evening I had one of those hours where the enchantment of the past falls over me once more. I saw the gulf waters silver under the moon. I saw old familiar red ploughed fields on a frosty autumn night, gardens by the sea that have in them something no inland gardens can ever have, beautiful young eyes that once looked upon those scenes with me. All about us, beyond the flickering light of the burning leaves was the strange deep sadness of a dead landscape on a late fall evening. But its darkness was peopled for me with the ghosts of a far land.

Then some of Stuart's chums came in and we had a corn roast. We sat on boxes around the fire and ate candy and roasted corn. Told jokes, sang community songs and had a very hilarious time. Why do things always taste so much better out of doors around a camp fire?

Then Ewan and I motored over to Union to make a call. As we spun along people were burning piles of potato stalks in the fields and the night seemed full of magic and engaging devilry. Bonfires in the dark are always pagan and belong to the old charming gods.

Something else belongs to them too—the thistles and mulleins along the road in the carlight. In the daylight they *are* thistles and mulleins. In carlight they are troops of Pan. Such eerie, gnomish things and creatures flashing up out of the shadows and sinking back again as we go by. They made our autumn roads at night a continuous procession through elfland.

By the way, we had a dreadful disappointment here one day in January 1925. For the first time in a very long period our section of Ontario was to have a total eclipse of the sun. Everybody was on tiptoe of expectation. Alas. Thick clouds covered the sky the whole forenoon. For a few moments everything was dark. That was all. We very sorrowfully put away our equipment of smoked glass for the next eclipse—which is due in about a hundred and thirty-five years or thereabouts!!

Last autumn in September of 1925 the first break in our little family circle came. Chester had to go away to school. He went to "St. Andrew's College"—really a collegiate or High School—and is back there this year. It was very hard for us all. We have grown used to it now of course—used to having only the one boy at home. Chester is almost as tall as his father and is in long trousers.

All the latter part of the year '24 and the first day of '25 were made unhappy for us by the terrible "Union" disruption in our Presbyterian church. Half of it went into Union, half stayed out. We remained Presbyterian, because we could not abide the coercive measures adopted by certain "leaders" who were determined to force the church into Union without giving the people a chance to say a word. Our congregation also voted Presbyterian. But some neighboring congregations were disrupted and it became necessary to make some new arrangements and to facilitate these Ewan decided that it would be best for us to move. So when Norval and Union "called" we listened.

It was bitterly hard to leave Leaskdale. We had been there 15 years. My boys were born there. It was *home*. Our people, too, were very unwilling to part from us. But we came; and now that the pain of parting is over and we are settled and pretty well acquainted we feel that we decided wisely.

Norval is a little village 30 miles out of Toronto, built in the valley of the Credit River. It is one of the beauty spots of Ontario and is really lovely. It is more like an old world village than a Canadian one. I love it already. All around it rise most beautiful hills of pines and maples and the views up and down the Credit are charming. Our people are very nice and our work pleasant. We have two congregations Norval and Union. (Union being the name of a community and having nothing to do with Church Union!) Our manse is a beautiful one and we are very comfortable and happy.

I enclose a few snaps which will give you a little idea of our new home and surroundings. This is a "short" letter as letters have been going with us lately. I could have written much more on various subjects of mutual interest but I want to get this letter mailed. As you say, shorter and more frequent letters are much better and I hope that after this we will not have these chilling gaps.

I ordered a copy of my new book *The Blue Castle* sent you. It's a little different from any of my others. The scene is laid, not in P. E. Island but in Muskoka. The reviewers seem very much divided over it. One says "the best story of year"—one says "Sentimental trash"—and there are all grades between!

Yours fraternally
L. M. Macdonald

The Manse
Norval, Ont.

Friday
Dec. 2/27.

Dear Mr. MacMillan:

I am sending to-day, in our annual exchange of books a copy of "Jalna,"[1] the novel by a Canadian girl which took the ten thousand dollar prize offered last spring by the Atlantic Magazine against fifteen hundred competitors. Of course Canada is "tickled" that a Canadian won. So I am sending it. I do not know whether you will like it. I can hardly say I did. Yet it is very brilliantly written. It certainly does *not* reflect life on the ordinary Canadian farm truly, I know that. But it is clever and "modern."

I hope you will have a pleasant and happy Christmastide. And I hope once the end of the year is over to find time to answer your letter.

Yours sincerely
L. M. Macdonald

1. *Jalna* is the first of the Whiteoak series by Mazo De la Roche.

The Manse
Norval, Ont.

Feb. 6/28

Dear Mr. MacMillan:
This is really an improvement. Here I am, answering, three months after receiving it and two months or more before the year is up since the date of my last. The world is certainly getting back to normal.

I have before me your letter and four short notes sprinkled through the summer. I have just re-read them all carefully and I shall reply to them first and foremost before I attempt to give you any "news" about my various doings and beings since last April.

I congratulate you on climbing Ben Lomond—and on being able to climb it. I feel quite sure I could not do it now, being fat and fifty, if not fair! *What* a view you must have had. "Could we but climb where Moses stood" was a hymn line that has always intrigued me. Oh, what the dwellers in the valleys miss, who never climb out of the valleys—spiritually, mentally, as well as physically.

Spiritually and mentally, I hope and believe, I have kept my love for high altitudes and my ability to attain them. But physically is a different story. I used to be such a walker. It is one of my keenest regrets that I can rarely ever do *any* walking now. I was afraid I had lost the power. And I was delighted when down home this summer to find that I could walk as well and as unweariedly as ever, despite forty added pounds of too too solid flesh. And walk I did, save at such times as the mistaken kindness of friends insisted on motoring me. Perhaps, if I attempted to climb Ben Lomond I might get another agreeable surprise and find I could but I doubt it.

· · ·

No, editors don't always know good stuff when they see it—good from a marketable point of view anyhow. Remember *Anne of Green Gables* was repressed five times before it was finally accepted.

Your second volume of Fay Inchfarm poems reached me in P. E. Island in July and were an added delight to my vacation. The day I received it I was wondering just what I would talk on that night at an Institute meeting I had rashly promised to address. Well, I just took that book along and read several of the poems and gave a rambling talk on the ideas they suggested to me. It "took" tremendously. I think the poem "Fools" despite its title is one of the most beautiful and appealing I have ever read. I have given it a great many times this past autumn and winter and it has always called forth delight and appreciation. Only once did it fail to register. I read it last week at a Women's Institute meeting and when I sat down the lady next to me said, "Oh, isn't that a cute little poem?"

I don't know whether you know the poem yourself, if not, try to read it somewhere, so you can savor the full bouquet of that "cute."

. . .

You ask in your letter if "Cavendish has become a place of pilgrimage for my admirers?" Alas, yes. And the chagrin expressed in that alas is not affectation at all but genuine regret and annoyance. Cavendish is being overrun and exploited and spoiled by mobs of tourists and my harmless old friends and neighbors have their lives simply worried out of them by car loads of "foreigners" who want to see some of Anne's haunts. I was down home a month this summer and there was hardly a day that was not spoiled for me by some such irruption. Some of them were journalists who went away and wrote their "impressions" in their papers, some of said impressions being very false and very annoying to my friends. I enclose one of them. To you, it will probably read all right; but to those who know the facts of the case there were many very annoying things in it. Not *all* the Cavendish people use the grammar of the farmer's wife in the article. The *Mrs. Warren* who poses in it as my early friend and helper was a schoolteacher who hated and persecuted me; and I returned the dislike. She does not know that she was the original of *Miss Brownell* in *New Moon* or she would not be quite so smug. (There, I've got it spelled right at last. That word always balls me up!) I remember the "rooster" incident very well—also the merciless calling down I received from her because of my "unladylike conduct." She quarrelled with my family and visited her resentment on me. And now! But what boots it? By an odd mistake the old Cavendish manse is listed as my old home!

And I was never in my life called "Lucy Maud." My friends called me "Maud" and nothing else.

.   .   .

As for the French not being particular what their "young girls" read, indeed they are! No nation of the world is so particular. The moment a French girl is married she can—and does—read anything and everything. But until she is married her reading is supervised meticulously. There are not many French books suitable for her, hence books like mine should really be a godsend to anxious "meres." By the way, they are now being translated into Polish.

No "In Veilage Haven" has nothing to do with "village." It really means, as I discovered only last week "In a Fair Haven." In the recent Dutch editions however they are calling it "Anne of The Green House" which is certainly nearer the original. I have not yet got a copy of *New Moon* in Dutch. When and if it comes (they do not always send one) I will copy the dedication for you. As to "the name of the unimaginable sweetness" which warned Emily that she was falling in love with Teddy, your question is difficult to answer because it's really one of the things one can't generalize about. It was once *my* experience. Yet, I can't say whether all or many girls experience just that particular sensation because I've never discussed it with any other girl—being "too Scotch" yet for that, even after five generations. Perhaps men couldn't have such an experience—perhaps only the more sensitive spiritual network of a woman could re-act in just that way.

.   .   .

I spent the month of July in P. E. Island. I had not been "down home" for three years and then only a brief trip to Aunt Annie's funeral. So it was really four years since I had been there for a vacation.

Again, as always when going back I was struck by the *brilliancy* of the Island. The amazing blue of its rivers—the amazing red of its roads—the amazing greenness of its trees and fields.

One day I had a delightful drive in a *buggy* with a friend. While, for this haste-mad age the auto is the only thing, it *is* a delight once more to get into a buggy behind a dreamy old horse and just *poke* along, driving for the sake of driving, in no hurry to get anywhere. We drove along red roads with daisies blooming on their banks, past little hollows full of scented fern, past old stone dykes festooned with wild strawberries, over looping blue rivers, by fields girdled by woods and through valleys where amber brooks called—and always the fragrance of dead fir coming with dear unexpectedness—that fragrance which is as the wine of old romance to me and always opens some flood-gate of my soul.

We passed a high hill covered with maples and my friend told me a tragic bit of local history which had happened seventy two years ago in her father's time. She had heard the story from him. Just beyond the hill was a hollow and in this hollow a woman of the neighborhood was found murdered. She had been stabbed with a knife and her face barbarously mutilated. The murderer—or *ess*—was never discovered. But there were suspicions. The murdered girl had been one of those "filles de joie" who are to be found everywhere; a certain man was known to be infatuated with her and his wife was half mad with jealousy. It was whispered—

Well, the body was taken to the schoolhouse that evening and by candlelight everybody in the community had to come to the school, lay his or her hand on the dead body and swear to innocence. It is hard to realize that this "ordeal" was practiced in P. E. Island only 72 years ago. But those old Highland emigrants retained old customs and superstitions generations after they had died out elsewhere. I myself have seen two old beldames who had the "second sight."

Among the rest came the suspected woman. Coolly and calmly she laid her hand on the mangled body and swore like the rest. The wounds of the dead light-o-love bled not. For no one's touch did they bleed. What a scene! The old superstitions might have been foolish indeed but with what drama they invested life. Is it well to grow too wise and scornful?

One day while there I got a letter from the Honorable Stanley Baldwin, Premier of Great Britain. A nice letter—a letter that made me purr. As it was very brief I will copy it here: 10 Downing St. "Dear Mrs. Macdonald: I do not know whether I shall be so fortunate during a hurried visit to Canada but it would give me keen pleasure to have an opportunity of shaking your hand and thanking you for the pleasure your books have given me. I am hoping that I shall be allowed to go to Prince Edward Island for I must see *Green Gables* before

I return home. Not that I wouldn't be at home at Green Gables!

I am yours sincerely
Stanley Baldwin

I took the letter with me to Lover's Lane and read it—read it not to myself but to the little girl who walked there years ago and dreamed—and wrote her dreams into books that have pleased a statesman of Empire. And the little girl was pleased!

One afternoon of my vacation seems to gleam out in memory like a jewel. It was a cool, pale-gray, fragrant day—the kind of day I love best—the kind of day we never have in Ontario. It belongs solely to the Maritimes. And I picked strawberries along the road the whole afternoon. The banks of the road and the old dykes were red with them. I was perfectly happy and—what is more than and distinct from happiness—perfectly *satisfied*. My *soul* was home. That afternoon alone was worth going to P. E. Island for.

One night I went down to the old sandshore where the young peoples "Group" were having camp-fire and told them stories of old days along that shore—among others the story of the Marco Polo. Have I ever told you this? If not let me know and I will tell it. It is well worth it.

The old Gulf is the same—"Time writes no wrinkle on its azure brow."

It was too dark to see the sea behind me but I could hear it. Gray ghost-mists were enfolding New London Harbor—the night was full of secrets and mysteries. Before me were the dunes lying in the weird shadows cast by the campfire. After the talk I had some chats with old friends while the young fry of 1927 flew about and served lunch. I knew very few of them; and I was not thinking of them. I was thinking of the young fry of 1897 who seemed lurking in the shadows outside the camp-fire circle. I swear I caught a glimpse of their faces now and again when a quick streak of flame shot up before they could dart back into 1897.

And I wished I were out there with them! Everytime I go back to Cavendish now I feel more acutely the sad truth of the old verse.

"Like mists that round a mountain gray
Hang for an hour then pass away.
So I and nearly all my race
Have vanished from my native place.
Each haunt of childhood's loves and dreams
More beautiful in fancy seems,
And if I to these scenes repair
I find I am a stranger there."

Speaking of looking over old books etc. I came across an old bound magazine of McClures Magazines in Cavendish of the vintage of '97. I looked it over with a sudden full realization of how the world had changed. One article intrigued me greatly. A sort of prophetic symposium of the views of many distinguished men as to what was going to happen in the next thirty years!!! Some prophesied wisely, some foolishly. And one said that before thirty years had passed war would be abolished— there would never be another great war—the world had grown too wise for it. Oh, did not the shadows of 1914 fall across his paper as he wrote?

One evening one of my friends complained that skunks were about and she feared for her chickens. Whereby hangs a grievous tale.

When I saw Anne of Green Gables in the movies some six years ago I was disgusted because in one scene she was depicted as picking up a skunk on the way to a picnic. And skunks were—then—absolutely unknown in P. E. Island. Never tell me that coming events do not cast their shadows before!

A few years ago when the fox boom was at its height in P.E.I. someone conceived the idea—may jackals sit on his grandmothers grave!—of starting a skunk ranch.

Accordingly the ranch was built and the skunks imported. The venture was a failure financially. And instead of dooming the skunks to death or exile they were simply turned loose with the fiendish result—that they are over-running the province. Moreover, an imbecile government has passed a law for their comfort and protection. They are not to be killed but allowed to replenish the earth. In spite of this indignant farmers *do* kill them. More power to their elbows. The fragrance of skunk on the crystal air of a P. E. Island summer evening is *not* a sweet savor unto the Lord.

When I came home the first of August I found an invitation to "meet His Royal Highness" at the Garden Party at Government House. So I fled me about to get a new dress and hat and went. It was very amusing and interesting. I never saw so many pretty dresses together in my life. (My own was passable. I shall send you a photo of it—with meself inside—some of these days). The Prince—I suppose you've seen him—was not the "smiling Prince" of the newspapers. He looked tired, bored, blasé, as no doubt he was and small blame to him. Prince George was far more chipper looking and seemed to be enjoying himself hugely, and I met and had a nice chat with Stanley Baldwin and Mrs. Baldwin who were both charming democratic folks. So that's that. I've put the gloves I wore when I shook hands with the Prince away as "heirlooms" for my grandchildren and much good may they do them.

Were you the correspondent who once asked me for a copy of the poem "Fate." At the time I could not find it but the other day it turned up. I am sending it herewith on the chance that it was you who asked for it. As I have no other copy will you please return it when you write.

I have been excessively busy this fall and winter. Besides everything else I am training two groups of young people in plays—one in Norval and one in Union. We did so well with our last play—making over $500 with it—that they all wanted to have another. But the work it makes!

I ask pardon for the blots on this page. They were not of my making. A small pussy cat with topaz eyes is the guilty party.

May 1928 be full of satisfaction and happiness for you.

Yours sincerely,
L. M. Macdonald

The Manse
Norval, Ont.

Feb 10/29

Dear Mr. MacMillan:

The Christmas "rush" is over, likewise the family dose of flu. So I am hoping now to get time to answer your letter—or letters—since there is a goodly number of notes as well as the main epistle in the pile before me. I shall not finish it to-day of course but a good beginning is half an ending—which is a proverb I invented all by myself.

.   .   .

Your clipping on "The Minister's Wife" was very pertinent. I never have to go to "Mothers Meetings," since they are unknown here but Mission Bands, Missionary Auxiliaries, Ladies Aids, Womens Institutes, Sunday School Teachers meetings etc. etc. etc. Sometimes I get so sick of them that I could hang myself on the handiest gooseberry bush rather than go to another. And yet its odd—it's always in prospect only that I hate them. When I get to them I find myself really quite enjoying them. I like "making things go," having, so I have been told, a "gift" that way. It is really only because of the inroads they make on my time that I rise up and howl over them occasionally.

137

Your next note bears the date of June 12, and accompanied the book "The Key Above the Door" which I found very delightful indeed. Oddly enough, I had been intrigued by a review I had read of it and had jotted it down on my list of books to be gotten. There is a wonderful freshness as of wind in heathery fields about it quite out of the common rut of modern fiction with its reeking atmospheres of brothel and latrine. Thank you very much for it.

The resemblance between Burns and his great etc. granddaughter is one of those things you couldn't believe if you didn't see them. It is marvellous—and after such a lapse of time, too. It renders quite probable the stories I have read of a certain face or form cropping out almost unchanged in families of long descent. I confess I have always felt very skeptical in regard to the probability or even possibility of this but I realize now that it is quite possible.

So you like *Blue Castle?* I loved Muskoka so much that for once I forsook my dear Island and laid the scene in Ontario. The Blue Castle was so successful that my publishers want me to write another in the same vein, so I am gathering together material for it. It is too chaotic yet to have or give any very clear idea of it but I think I'll make it centre around the adventures of an old heirloom jug in a clan, the members of which all want to fall heir to it.

.   .   .

I had only a week's brief vacation last summer but I really packed a month's enjoyment into it. We left home one Monday morning and motored to Orillia—from there on through Muskoka, as far as Sundridge. We had a delightful day of beautiful scenery. Tuesday morning we motored to North Bay and from there through sixty miles of virgin forest where the new "Ferguson Highway"—called after Ontario's present premier—cuts through the Government Timber reserve, where real wild bears live! We did see a bear cub. Every moment was a delight and the greatest delight of all was the innumerable lakes starred with water lilies, the most exquisite things blooming there in that wilderness—untouched and untouchable—for they never grow within reach and unless you have a boat you can not get them. One must look at them—desire them—and pass on. Have you wild water lilies in Scotland?

We went as far as New Liskeard that night—passing through Cobalt where mines of richness are—gold, silver, nickel. Such a desolate unlovely town surrounded by ghastly leprous hills. I could not live a week in such a place if I discovered a new silver mine every morning. In the morning we turned homeward and reached Sundridge again that night. Somehow that night stands out in memory as a particularly lovely one. The little hotel on Lake Bernard was full. So we had to sleep in a tiny cabin right down on the sandy shore by the lake. Before I went to bed I sat alone for an hour on a log out on a little sandy point in the dreamy August twilight. To my left was a beautiful little cove where the shadows of the trees in the rose and silver water were even lovelier than the trees themselves. I held communion again with my dear friend the night after the fashion of old years. The darkness was like a cool draught to drink—some magic brew that for a little space brought youth back. I was lapped round by an exquisite silence, and I slept in that little cabin room as I have not slept for a long long time—slept soundly, dreamlessly refreshingly and woke in the early morning to bathe my soul in dawn and love the mists that hung over the lake. There the sun came out and performed its old miracle; the beautiful lake horizons emerged from the silver glamour; and I turned away from it regretfully as one always parts from a fleeting glimpse of beauty one will not see again.

The next afternoon we reached Begwin Inn and stayed there 24 hours. I think I sent you a card from there. I have been in many hotels and summer resorts but never in any that delighted me so much as Begwin Inn. We came home next day.

In September my baby left me. When Chester returned to St. Andrew's College Stuart went with him. Our house was left unto us desolate. It is useless to describe how lonely we were—and are. Of course they get home for frequent holidays but one must face the fact that they *are* holidays—and that never again will they be really *living* at home.

In October I contrived to finish and pack off to the publishers my new book "Magic for Marigold." It is about a little girl but some of the chapters may interest an adult.

We had an "Old Time Night" in our Young Peoples Guild this winter—old songs, old recitations, old costumes. I hired one for the night from a Toronto house and went in "a costume of Mary Queen of Scots." Believe me, I made quite a sensation. It was a gorgeous affair. A skirt of crimson velvet trimmed with gold braid, ermine and ropes of pearls; a bodice of velvet with a "diamond" stomacher, more pearls and loose hanging sleeves of yellow lace. *And* a ruff of lace besprinkled with diamonds and edged with pearls. A devilish thing to wear but *very* becoming. I wore a "diamond" crown and recited "Mary Queen of Scots."

It is curious—the effect clothes have on us psychologically. When I put on that dress I *was* Mary of Scotland—and I hated to put it off—in spite of the fact that its weight was simply tremendous. But it *felt* so rich and splendid and romantic.

And now I am going to expound a dark secret which I promised should be revealed to you in the fulness of time. You remember your surprise when you found on Harrap's list of my books a certain one "Further Chronicles of Avonlea" which you never knew existed. Well, thereby hangs a tale—a tale that would fill a volume but must be condensed into a few pages. For the past *nine years* my existence has been to a certain extent a nightmare because of "Further Chronicles."

As you know L. C. Page Co. of Boston were my first publishers. They were *crooks* but I did not know this. When they accepted *Anne of Green Gables* (because a P.E.I. girl on their staff gave them no peace till they did) they asked me if I would prefer a royalty or a certain sum outright. I know now they thought I would jump at "the certain sum" in which case I would have got $500 for *Green Gables.* But green as I was I was not so green as that so I said "a royalty." The contract was a hard one even for a beginner and one clause in it was that I must give them all my books on *the same terms* for a period of five years. I did not think this mattered because I never dreamed Green Gables was going to be a big success so I willingly signed up.

In 1912 I had no new book ready so the Pages asked me to send them all my short stories for a volume to fill in. I sent them all I had of any value at all. They selected the best and "Chronicles of Avonlea" were published. They sent back the rest but *unknown to me kept copies of them.* I destroyed the MSS. they returned as I did not think they would ever be needed again. I must say that I had rewritten all the stories largely and added a good deal of new material mostly descriptive. These new descriptive bits I kept and used them from time to time in the various books that followed—The Golden Road, Anne of the Island etc. etc. This is an important point— keep it in memory.

By 1916 I found it impossible to carry on with the Page Co. any longer. All their authors had left them and I was compelled to do so too. The time limit had now expired so I went to Stokes. Page was furious and threatened lawsuits to no end but in the end he did nothing because he hadn't the shadow of a claim anywhere.

The next year he kept back $1000 out of my royalties

on the ground that I had been overpaid previously. I needn't go into these details. Page's record is full of these things when dealing with his women writers. He did no end of crooked things because he knew most women would submit to anything rather than go to law. But I come of a different breed of cats. I got the Authors League of America to find me a good Boston lawyer, Mr. Rollins, and I entered suit in 1919 and won it. The judge gave me the $1000 dollars.

Page had now found out there was no chance of bulldozing me and his lawyer Mr. Way (a very fine man by the way) approached me with an offer to buy my rights in the books entirely out. I was as anxious to get rid of them as they were to be rid of me, so I named a sum which would bring me in as much income every year if permanently invested as the royalties on the books were. After long dickering they came up to my price but on one condition. They asked me to allow them to publish another volume of short stories—those stories they had returned in 1912. This is where I made my mistake. I should never have done it. But I was terribly worried at the time, having just got word of the fatal illness of my dear friend Frede Campbell in Montreal and I wanted to get away at once and be free, as I fondly fancied of the Page Co. for evermore.

Besides they insinuated a vague threat that they could get those stories from the original magazines and publish them any time they liked—the very year I was bringing out a new book perhaps. So, as the stories were poor stuff, I agreed. I was to send copies of the stories. Of course being bound to Stokes I had to get their consent which they freely gave *on condition that there would be no mention of Anne* in the book. So the contract was drawn up and the Pages given the right to publish the book in 1920. I went home, sent them copies of the stories and thought no more about them.

Then in the fall of 1919 Page wrote me that they had

"discovered in their vaults copies of the stories I had sent in 1912 and were going to publish *them* as the contract gave them the right to do." I was aghast. Not only were there pages of description in those old Ms. that by this time had been used in succeeding books but there were several appearances of Anne in them—inserted when I was preparing them for possible inclusion in the first "Chronicles." This meant a breach of my contract with Stokes and would lay me open to breach of contract suit from them if they wanted to be nasty. Also I would be made absurd by a book coming out under my name containing no end of paragraphs and descriptions which were to be found in my other books.

I got Mr. Rollins to notify Page that they had no right to publish the 1912 versions and I would bring suit against them if they did. But they did it and brought out "Further Chronicles" in March 1920. I at once brought suit for an injunction against the book and damages to my literary reputation. The case came up in May 1920. I went down to Boston for it. Page's lawyer thought the case would be over in *two days*. My lawyer was not so optimistic and thought it would take three. *It took nearly nine years!*

Page's regular lawyer would not take the case so they got a Mr. French—a very able fellow and a very unscrupulous one. By the time two days were over it became evident that it was going to be longer than they thought. So it went before a "Master." This Master hears the evidence at leisure, gives his opinion thereon and hands it to the judge who decides accordingly.

I had to stay in Boston until the middle of July. I was on the witness stand for *three weeks* on end, being cross-examined by the ablest lawyer at the Boston bar. Can you fancy a more nerve-wracking ordeal. But I was telling the truth and not afraid to tell it and he could not break me down. You have heard no doubt of "the maddening delays of the law." Well, I know all about them. The hardest thing was French's "trick" questions. But, "though I say it as hadn't orter" he never trapped me once. And when it came to *my* lawyer's turn to grill the Page brothers we got some fun out of it—for *they* were lying and worried and would get all tangled up and contradict themselves and each other.

Of course the whole thing hinged on the interpretation of the contract and French dragged in something every day to befog the issue. One day Mr. Rollins got George Page to admit a certain thing and after the session he said to me "We've won our case, I was afraid we couldn't get him to admit that."

But we were a long way from winning it. The lawyers would spend *hours* wrangling over the admissibility of certain questions or evidence and for days we would make no progress at all that I could see. Just think of my worry. And one of my boys ill at home! And yet that battle of wits between trained intellects was amazingly fascinating and if I had not been the toad under the harrow I would have enjoyed it. *One whole day* those three lawyers and myself wrangled over the exact color of *Anne's* hair and the definition of "Titian" red. Ye, gods it *was* funny. The big table was snowed under with literature and prints to disprove or prove. They had two "art experts" on the stand who flatly contradicted each other. Years before when I sat down in that old house in Cavendish one rainy evening and dowered Anne with red tresses I did not dream that a day would come when it would be fought over in a Boston court-room. French was determined to prove that Titian hair was dark red and that I knew it was dark red. I didn't. I always supposed it was a sort of flame red and I stuck to it through all his badgerings. One expert said it was "bright golden-auburn" and the other said it was the color of burnished coffee. And so on!

The raison d'etre of all this was the picture of the red-headed girl on the cover which was a part of our case.

By the end of June the Pages evidently thought that the case was not going to be over as soon as they had hoped and decided to hurry it up a bit by scaring me into dropping it. They handed me a writ, suing me for $30,000 damages for libel because of the statements in my "bill of complaint." This was absurd of course. A bill of complaint is privileged and they had no case. But the trouble is in the States you have to pay your own fees and costs whether you win or lose and the wealthy Page Co. could afford that better than I could. But my fighting mood was up and I was determined to ignore their threat and fight to the end. Still, you can imagine the worry and vexation this inflicted on me.

Then a Page witness swore to a flat lie—a most damaging lie to our case and my lawyer lost his grit. He said it was such damaging testimony that he thought we'd better offer to settle. I would *not* knuckle down to the Pages after the way they had behaved and said so. So on we went.

I came home in mid July a perfect wreck. But the case went on.

In September French filed his damage suit for the libel. Then the Master took *nearly a year* to make up his report. In September 1921 it came—and it was decidedly adverse to us. I had never expected anything else, of course, after the lies the Pages swore to—and he believed. The report was sent to the judge but it is a *very* rare thing that a judge does not follow the Master's findings. As for the libel suit in August 21 it was thrown [out] of the Massachusetts court on the ground that it was illegal. Then Page appealed it to the Supreme Court of the State. In six months it was thrown out there. Then he carried it to the Supreme Court of the United States!

As for the Masters report handed in in September 1921 would you believe it was April 1923 before the judge gave his decision. Such a thing was never heard of

145

I believe. But perhaps it was as well for me because what happened was that the judge discarded the Master's report and examined all the evidence himself. There was about a trunkful of typewritten evidence and he told Mr. Rollins he had never met such an interesting case in his life. *And he gave decision in my favor.* I got my injunction against the book and *all* the profits.

Oddly enough the very same day word came that the Page appeal had been thrown out by the Supreme Court of the U.S.

Do you think my worry was over then! Not by a jugful! Of course the Pages at once appealed from the judge's decision.

And in December 1923 they filed the same old libel suit in the courts of *New York State* and attached my royalties due from Stokes to compel me to fight the case over again there. A New York lawyer had to be engaged also!

In June 1924 the New York suit was dismissed. Then Page appealed to the Supreme Court of New York.

On March 4, 1925, the appeal in my case was decided in my favor.

Then they had to begin the "accounting" to find out what the "Profits" really were.

In October 1925 the New York libel case was finally thrown out and my long withheld royalties paid to me. My N.Y. lawyer wrote me that, since I was not a resident of N.Y. state I had a clear case against the Page Co. for the repayment of all the N.Y. suit had cost me. It had cost me $2,000. So I thought I would show Page I had plenty of fight left in me yet and I at once entered suit in New York against him!

In June 1927 the judge gave decision on the profits in my favor. The Pages' appealed the amount. In March 1928 I won my New York suit and got back my money.

And *finally* in October 1928 the Page appeal was refused. *At last* there was nothing more they could do by hook or crook. They paid me $18,000 of profits and the thing was ended after nearly 9 years of worry and expense. The suit cost me $15,000. So I had for recompense $3,000, my injunction against the book—*and* the satisfaction of having rebuffed the Pages to a finish!

The suit cost the Pages about $75,000 in all. And for the last four years they and their lawyer French have not been on speaking terms, though he continued to act for them.

Those are just the outlines! The details would fill a library!

I'm sure you would like to have a copy of the historic book over which such a tremendous legal battle was fought. So I'll send you a copy as soon as I've time to mark it explanatorily. The day may come when it will be of value as a curio—(when my diary is published! Your heirs may benefit if not you).

I began this letter Feb. 10. It is now March 10—and spring—and house-cleaning. But, thank God, *no lawsuits!*

Yours fraternally,
L. M. Macdonald

The Manse
Norval, Ont.

Dear Mr. MacMillan:

I have not put any date at the beginning of this letter. I shall put in the date when I finish it, if I ever do! I shall not make a single excuse or apology. I shall just begin.

I have always been a systematic devil. And I find that the vice—I really do fear it *is* a vice—is obtaining a more and more powerful hold on me as I grow older. It has invaded my letters. I have to write them systematically, too. Hence I shall open my correspondence notebook,

ascertain the date of my last letter to you, open my journal at that date and proceed to tell you any bit of news
or philosophy or fun that may turn up in proper se-
quence. That done I shall take your unanswered letters
with their batches of clippings and make such comments
thereupon as may seem good unto me. Selah.

.　　.　　.

Here is a July entry that may be of interest. "Sunday,
July 14, 1929. To-night I had a divine half hour when
my soul was filled and satisfied with beauty, desiring
nothing else.

I was alone in the manse reading Herodotus (I think I
would have liked Herodotus very much by the way. He
is really an old duck!) I went out, slipped up the street in
the magic hour of mingled twilight and moonshine,
across Russell's field pasture and so up to the hill of
pines. There I roamed for an exquisite space that was
only half an hour by the clock but which seemed a sort
of lifetime by some other computation. The lingering
hues of a wonderful sunset were still staining the sky
over another dark pine hill to the west of me. Lights of
unending cars were swooping jewel-like around the
curve of the highway far below me. Silence seemed to
come through the pines to me like a Real Presence—
hovering, enfolding, blessing. Those great tall trees
around me were my brothers—my older wiser brothers.
I stood for many minutes by one of them, my arm
around it, my face pressed to it, breathing a prayer to
the God of Beauty I have always served—a new reconse-
cration to Him. Fresh from Herodotus, I felt like the
priestess of an oracle under her sacred pines. When I finally came reluctantly away I said, '*This* Sunday at least
has been a *holy* day for me.' I feel rested—re-created. I
shall sleep tonight. The utter calm of that grove has possessed me."

We were, through no fault of our own at all, involved

in two nasty automobile casualties in July, neither of which helped to restore my jangling nerves.

Have you seen—or heard—the "talkies." The first one I heard last August. During the first third I did not like it—the effort to hear what was being said interfered with my enjoyment. Then I suddenly found it easy to hear and enjoyed the rest. But I doubt if I shall ever like the "talkies" as well as the silent pictures. I like the "legitimate drama" and I like a good picture but I don't care for the mixture.

New inventions crowd on each others heels—each more amazing than the last. But the trouble is—no one is happier or better because of them.

August 11, 1929

This morning by way of variety we had a little earthquake. About half past six I awakened with the sensation that a big dog was padding heavily about the room. The whole house seemed to be full of knocks and queer noises. A dozen men seemed to be dancing on the zinc roof overhead. One of them was performing a *pas seul* on the bay window roof outside my room. An enormous truck seemed to be rumbling past. I sprang out of bed and drew up the shade. There was no truck—no dancer—no dog. Chester called out from his room to quit knocking—he was up. (He thought I was the knocker.) Then I suddenly realized what it was. The noise and tremor lasted about 20 seconds. This is the third earthquake shock I have experienced since I came to Ontario. Up in Brampton, seven miles away, the paper on the walls in many houses was cracked.

I had quite a sick spell in August and early in September Stuart had to have his tonsils out. Then friends came from P. E. Island and we had a delightful but pretty strenuous two weeks. And I find in my journal a

149

delightful story my friend told me. It's too good to be wasted so here's to pass it on.

Long ago when Fannie was a girl on her father's farm at Milton, P. E. Island, her step-sister Sarah lived there too. The said Sarah had a beau named Lem McLean. And the said Sarah did not want a beau named Lem McLean. So the said Sarah turned the said Lem down one night, coldly and flatly and irrevocably. Now, good industrious Mr. Wise (my friend's father) had spent that whole day planting a hedge of young spruce trees up and down both sides of his long lane. It was a hard day's work and no doubt he surveyed the results at nightfall with pardonable pride—"something attempted, something done, had earned a night's respose." But while Mr. Wise slumbered and slept the rejected Lemuel was walking down the lane seething with impotent rage of soul. It had to be vented in some way. So Lem, as he stalked along, grabbed up a handful of the young spruces, first on one side and then on the other, all the way down the lane to the road. No doubt it did him heaps of good. But when poor Mr. Wise arose in the morning his nice little hedges were a series of gaps!!

History does not record what Mr. Wise did—or said. It would probably not have become a loyal daughter to reveal. He never found time to fill up the gaps. The trees grew up and are now, Fanny says, as big and tall as 40 year old spruces can be. But every few yards there is a tell-tale space reminiscent of that frenzied swain—who has been wedded for years to another lady and perhaps has completely forgotten how he wreaked his passion on Mr. Wise's spruce hedge!!

As a rule, I do not feel any mad desire to go out and yank up somebody's trees. But there have been times when I could sympathize with Lem McLean—not because of unrequited affection but just out of impatience with the general cussedness of things.

150

By September I concluded I had to have a vacation or bust. So I went down to "the Island." I had never seen it in its autumn coloring since I had married and I longed to see it again. Would I find the old charm? I did. Doubled and trebled. And I had such a wholly delightful and satisfying vacation that I was just a little afraid. The gods do not give gifts like that for nothing.

The first Sunday night I was home we drove to Cherry Valley. Isn't that a delightful name? The drive was a sheer delight. The rain of the day had ceased. The sun had come out and performed its usual miracle on those blue harbors and winding red roads. When it set a great orange moon was rising over fields of wheat "stooks." Lights were twinkling out here and there through the lovely, pale, clear autumn dusk. The Sunday evening "sacred concert" was pleasant. And when we came out after it I stood entranced on the steps of the Cherry Valley church—which is "beautiful for situation." There before me was once more the beauty of a moonlit sea—the lovely Pownal Bay, a dream of silver and shadow. I just stood there and fed my soul on it while I talked to friends—and the boys were running around in the crowd, cutting out their girls and steering them off to the waiting cars—just as in olden years, only it was buggies then.

I motored up to Cavendish from Charlottetown with friends one mellow Sunday afternoon. I had been telling my friends the Lem McLean story and, as we were to pass the old Wise place, Albert declared he would make an excuse to call and find if we could see the trees—or what was left of them. We drove in to it by a new treeless lane. It is now owned by a family named Gillespie. The lady of the house came out to the car and Maud introduced me, winding up with a little flourish about "L. M. Montgomery."

No response appeared on Mrs. Gillespie's very stolid

face. Poor Maud saw that her bit of lion parading had fallen flat and, not having enough sense to leave the thing alone, persisted,

"Haven't you read any of her books?" Mrs. G. fixed on me a blank uninterested stare.

"No," she said. "Is she a Baptist?"

All the way to Cavendish we argued over what she meant. I thought perhaps she was under a vow not to read anything save what was written by a Baptist. Albert opined that she thought nobody but a Baptist could write anything worth reading. Maud said it was likely she just thought I looked like a Baptist!

Albert told Mrs. G. the story of the lane but, like Queen Victoria of blessed memory, she was not amused. She said they had closed up the lane and cut all the trees down. So that was that.

When we reached Cavendish we drove down to the shore. Some Sunday tourists were there and one of them, a rugged old Irishman who looked as if he had never opened a book in his life, came up to me and exclaimed, "Shure an' I niver dreamed I'd have the honour of shaking hands wid ye. I've read ivery book ye've iver writan. I hope ye'll live for a hundred years and kepe on writing them. Ye're the bright star of Prince Edward Island and we're all proud of ye."

It takes an Irishman to put the blarney over. He was quite a nice antidote to Mrs. Gillespie!

I had a beautiful two weeks in Cavendish. The weather was exquisite. I played with charming Island kittens—I roamed for hours in gold and crimson Island woods—I prowled about the silver shore. I visited old friends and ate chicken dinners—surely the Island hens would be thankful when I left. And I spoke one evening for an Institute meeting and after it was over a gaunt old farmer, aged 84, came up and shook my hand fervently.

"I want to tell you that I once *went home with your mother,* " he said!!

The last evening of my stay Alec and May Macneill[1] and I spent with two other friends "Bob and Jennie" who live in a little white house on a hill. The five of us sat down together in a little parlor which probably transgressed every canon of "modern" good taste but nevertheless continued to be a very cozy, home-like little spot, and bandied jokes and insults all the evening, laughing till the tears literally ran down our faces. Every one of us *could* laugh. There are people who can't. Nice people, too—who smile and enjoy themselves but can never let themselves go in unashamed howls and yells of mirth. Oh Bob and Alec and May and Jennie and I "made whoopee" all right that October night, while the rain poured down outside and a wild northeast wind bellowed over the gulf.

On my way home I stumbled by accident on the solution of a mystery that has long puzzled me. In 1921 or thereabouts *Green Gables* was in the movies. Mary Miles Minter as *Anne* scored a tremendous success. It put her definitely on the map; the movie world was at her feet and everyone predicted a career for her rivalling Mary Pickford. Then, all at once, Mary Minter simply disappeared and was never heard of again on the screen. Not only that, but every film in which she had starred faded promptly out of existence. "Anne" after its successful year in the big theatres, never had the usual second year in the "uptowns" and although it was "billed" in Great Britain and Australia was never actually shown there. I often wondered over this but never could solve the mystery.

In Montreal station I was prowling about looking for something to read on the day-long ride to Toronto and I found a book with the cheerful title "Twelve Unsolved

1. To whom L.M. dedicated *Pat of Silver Bush.*

153

Murder Mysteries." Half way through it I found the tale of the murder of William Desmond Taylor.

The said Taylor had directed the picture of *Anne.* He was a handsome and fascinating man, living in Hollywood, apart from his wife and had had many love affairs. Mary Miles Minter was infatuated with him. One morning Taylor was found dead on the floor of his Hollywood bungalow. He had been shot. It has never been discovered who murdered him. I don't think the golden curled Mary was suspected, although another film star was, but when the police took possession of his bungalow several things were discovered which doomed poor Mary in the eyes of the virtuous American public more fatally than even murder would have done. Among other matters, a packet of letters from her to Taylor, showing conclusively that Mary had loved the handsome movie magnate not wisely but too well. This ended her career on the silver sheet. The company that had had a contract with her bought her off with a huge sum and all the films in which she had starred went into oblivion with her. One can't help feeling sorry for poor Mary who committed the unpardonable sin of being found out.

.　　.　　.

Yes, the Flower Patch Neighbors came safely and I did enjoy it tremendously. I was immensely intrigued to find that the incident of Valency's getting her foot caught in a railroad was duplicated in "He Comes Up Smiling." I have never heard either of the novel or the writer. Would it be possible for you to get a copy of it and send it to me? I will of course fork up the cash for it. Or if it was published this side of the pond tell me the name of the publisher and I will get it myself. I do not think, however, that it is exactly what might be called a co-incidence. My incident was taken from life. A few

154

years ago in Chicago a man & his wife were walking to church through a railway yard. The lady got her shoe caught just as Valency did. Her husband seeing he could not release her caught her in his arms and died with her, both killed by the impact of the train. The American and Canadian papers were filled with it and reams of letters and editorials were written, discussing the ethics of the husband's action, especially as I seem to remember he had a son and daughter at home. Likely Mr. Sherman read of this, as I did, and worked it into his novel.

Yes, wasn't the cover design of *Marigold* delightful— in spite of the old moon.

I am busy now on a "grown-up" humorous novel, which will not however be ready for publication before 1931.

. . .

Stuart was very much delighted with those beautiful crests you sent. He has really quite an interesting collection.

Here are the answers to your questions regarding my lawsuit with the Page Co.

The words "Presentation Copy" simply mean that it was one of the complimentary copies sent to the author.

Most of the copies of the book published were sold long before the case was concluded. The unsold ones (a few) became my property. The Page Co. had to pay me all the profit on the book.

Yes, it was malice that made Page use his copies. He hoped to embroil me with my new publishers because their consent to my letting him have the stories was conditioned on the assurance that there would be nothing about *Anne* in them.

Thanks for the volume of Fay Inchfarm's poems. Everything she writes has a charm for me.

March 31, 1930

I think I have written up pretty nearly all the items of interest available so I shall conclude this epistle. By the way your colored leaves came in very good shape, not much—I think—dimmed. Lucky has just touched a paw to this sheet. He must be sending you a greeting.

Yours cordially,
L. M. Macdonald

The Manse
Norval, Ont.

March 15/31

Dear Mr. MacMillan:

Have you ever lived through a year during which no great calamity overtook you but which was one unbroken succession of petty worries, stings, annoyances, disappointments, and vexations. Such has been this past year for me. It has been absolutely unique in my experience. Hardly one of the various tribulations *in itself* was worth speaking of or worrying over; but when it was multiplied by a thousand it was a different matter. *One* mosquito sting is bearable; but an endless succession of mosquito stings is, I believe, harder on the nerves and more destructive of ordinary everyday happiness than breaking a leg or having an operation for appendicitis. However, all this is merely by way of explanation, not complaint. We all have to "take our lumps."

· · ·

In October last I took a trip out west. I do not know if I have ever happened to mention that *forty years ago* I spent a year in Prince Albert, Saskatchewan, with my father and his second wife. I went to school there and made several friendships which I have always kept up, but I have never been back since. The trip out was rather tedious as I went by the C.N.R. which runs through the pulp woods of northern Ontario. The first day was really the most tedious I ever spent in travelling. From dawn to dark we saw absolutely nothing save endless leagues of young spruce and birch. I passed the day reading a bundle of "John O'London's" which had come just as I left home and I tossed it into my suit case. They really saved my reason. And when I had read every word in them I worked the cross-word puzzles. I adore cross-word puzzles and hardly ever have time to do one: So I had a real devilish orgy of it that day. And in addition I found a thing of beauty in a verse of Poe's which I never saw before. It was so exquisite it hurt me. And yet I can't explain *why* it was so exquisite. It was one of those verses which seem to hold for me some secret, mysterious magic, quite apart from the ideas expressed.

"Now all my days are trances
And all my nights are dreams
Of where thy dark eye glances
And where thy foot step gleams
In what ethereal dances
By what eternal streams."

The special magic is in the last two lines. I repeated them over and over again as the train sped along and every time the thrill of spiritual ecstacy they gave me was so acute as to be almost anguish. Why—*why*? Did *I* ever share in some "ethereal dance" by "some eternal stream" and was it a pang of divine homesickness that rent my soul? At all events, the couplet rainbowed the day for me and will sing to me forever. For which take my heart-felt thanks, since it was you who sent me John O' London.

I spent a day in Winnipeg on my way out west and

had of course to revise my 40-year-old impressions of it. The changes were enormous.

Next day at noon I reached Saskatoon. Just before we got to it a porter went through the car proclaiming sonorously "Time goes back an hour." But for me it went back forty years!

I was met at Saskatoon by a woman[1] who had been a most dear and intimate school friend during that western year. I had dreaded meeting her. Would I find a stranger?

And I found her—no stranger but the same dear "kindred soul."

I suppose we made dreadful fools of ourselves on that public platform. We were really quite mad. But

"There is a pleasure keen in being mad
Which none but madmen know."

We would embrace and kiss—draw back—look at each other—embrace again. I don't know how long we kept that up. Time had ceased to have any meaning for us. I have never in all my life felt just such an extraordinary emotion as I experienced then. I would not exchange those moments for the Ho-i-noor. I knew then that love was immortal.

"Is it *you*," I said. "Is it *you*?" said she. It was!

Our brief insanity passed but we simply revelled in each other for a week.

When I saw Saskatoon last it was a station, a post office & store, and five shacks. *Now* it is a city of 30,000!

Laura and I *talked*, night and day. It seemed impossible to catch up with 39 years of talk in seven days but we accomplished it after a fashion, leaping from year to year with incredible agility.

Of course we told no end of stories. Here is a priceless one Laura told me—about an old character she had known in early Prince Albert days; named—or nicknamed—"Skilly McLeod." The said Skilly was noted for

1. Laura (Pritchard) Agnew, to whom L.M. dedicated *Anne's House of Dreams*.

his "Spoonerisms." One stormy spring night a flood swept away a mill-dam pertaining to his brother Angus. The next morning the Bishop happened to call and found old Skilly rushing around in wild excitement. "Oh, Good Lord, my morning, Good Lord, my morning, you'll excuse our being a bit upset here. My dam brother Angus burst in the night"!!!!

The first morning after my arrival in Saskatoon I was out in the garden with Laura's son. He glanced up and said "The air mail is two hours late." There was the plane—soaring through the blue sky. I realized *then* that it was forty years since I had been in "the great lone land." There is *no* "great lone land" now.

Here is a "co-incidence" which you will find it hard to believe. One evening Laura and I were alone and I said to her, "Laura, what has become of your old beau, George Gunn?" The said George was a divinity student in P.A. forty years ago and quite mad about sixteen year old Laura. She said she didn't know—she had never seen him or heard about him since that summer. She had hardly uttered the words when there was a ring at the bell. Laura went to the door—and on the step stood George Gunn!

No, of course you won't believe it. It is too much to ask of human credulity!

Nevertheless, it is *true*. He was passing through Saskatoon, heard Laura was living there and looked her up. The gods threw me in for good measure!

My week in Saskatoon ended Laura and I both went to P.A. and spent a week—a most hilarious week—with a mutual old chum there.

Prince Albert was also changed out of all recognition. Once a frontier town of about 1000 it is now a town of 15,000. The corner where father's house stood is built over as part of a business block. But I saw ghosts everywhere. The hills along the river where I picked hazel nuts and strawberries are now streets of residences. The river was almost the only thing unchanged. In my day the streets were full of Indians, squaws & pappooses [sic]. This time I did not see a single Indian!

I heard a delicious yarn at a reception I attended. A lady came up to me and told me her husband was a High School teacher who had told her to be sure to tell me this tale. In a certain exam paper on English History he had asked his class to name the wives of Henry the Eighth. In one paper the answer began as follows. "Katherine of Aragon, Anne of Green Gables, Jane Seymour etc."!!!

One day I went to the cemetery and stood by father's grave. This is an experience not to be written of. I loved my father very very deeply. He was the most lovable man I ever knew. He died in 1900.[2]

After leaving P.A. I visited several other towns, including Edmonton and had an enjoyable time but no *rest*. So that when I came home the first of November I was rather tireder than when I started. And I don't seem to have got rested since.

About three weeks ago I had my fifth attack of flu—a very bad one and it has left me in bad shape. But one thing it did do for me. For a week after I got up I could do nothing but lie around—so I fell to and read *all* your letters over, from the first to the last. And let me tell you, they stood the test well. They were as interesting as ever. But they made me realize the passage of time as nothing else has done.

I am going to ask a question which may evoke painful recollections. If *too* painful ignore it. In a letter written in 1917 you made your last reference to *Miss Allan*.[3] You

2. Hugh John Montgomery was born in Park Corner, P.E.I. in 1841.
3. Jean Allan, a friend of George MacMillan, who vacationed with MacMillan and the Macdonalds in 1911 in Scotland. (See pp. 62 and 85 for brief references to her.)

said she was married to a man who was then serving in some war organization—I forget the letters. What has become of her? Does she live in Alloa? Do you ever meet her?

It is time to close this letter, since I have "caught up" with the events of the year. I hope when I next write I will feel a wee bit more like living. I forgot to say that I finished my new book about New Year's and sent it to the publisher. For the first time in my life I have not been able to christen a brain-child. Nor have my publishers been more successful. We can't find a suitable name. It is "different" from anything I've done yet. Intended to be a *humorous* adult novel. *I* want to call it "Crying For The Moon." My publishers think that suggests a problem novel rather than a humorous one. So the matter hangs. I feel too tired to care much.

Yours fraternally
L. M. Macdonald

Happy New Year

Sunday
Jan 1, 1933

Dear Mr. MacMillan:

.   .   .

Recently I re-read "Dr. Thorne" and "Framley Parsonage" by Trollope—and was consoled. The world is upside down. All our cherished beliefs and traditions have gone by the board. Red Russia's shadow lies darkly over all. But thank God it is still possible to read Anthony Trollope. Do you know him at all?

.   .   .

161

Did Edison's death affect you? I thought of the Bible verse "A Prince and a great man has fallen this day in Israel."

I suppose Edison and Henry Ford have done more to change the world than any other two men since the birth of history. Only the unknown man who first conceived the idea of making a picture stand for a word on the shoulder blade of a deer or a bit of bark can be classed with them.

During several weeks of the past year when I was ill and worried and *blue* I re-read all those "Flower Patch" books you have sent me. They soothed and rested and cheered me. I cannot tell how much. Surely that is the proper function of literature in a world like this!

Did you follow that Lindbergh baby case? It was a hellish thing. That poor mother!

And what about God?

Young Stuart has been going in for gymnastics this last year. He is Junior champion for Ontario and won the gold medal at the Toronto Exhibition in September for the parallel bars against all Canada. He passed his Junior matric. last year and is now in his last year at St. Andrew's. Chester is in his second year in mining engineering. They are both grown. Did *we* grow up so fast?

About two weeks ago I finished my new book "Pat of Silver Bush." It is a story for girls, of the *Anne* and *Emily* type and will probably please that public. I wrote it against time and tide and have no great expectations for it.

I spent October on my dear Island and had a very lovely restful time. Some of it sad. Many old friends gone beyond the veil since my last visit. Many changes. But the old gulf is still the same and I saw a real storm on it once more. People there have not forgotten how to live. They have still time for sweet simple things. My sojourn there did me so much good. I came home rested and better in every way. *And* I took my movie camera down with me and a 100 ft. film and got some splendid pictures. When I came home and had them developed and ran them through the kodascope they had the most uncanny effect on me. I can hardly describe it. It seemed to me that I was *looking through a window* right on P. E. Island. There was a friend walking towards me with the waves rolling in at her feet—there was the spray of the surf tossing over the rocks—there was Lover's Lane—and dozens of other friends laughing and talking before me. It seemed as if they *must* hear me if I just *called* to them. And it made me frightfully home-sick. At one home where I stayed they had *five* beautiful cats and it was a sight to see them fed. I got a splendid "movie" of them. And there were some moonlit nights over the gulf! "Art, glory, freedom fall, but Nature still is fair."

I think I have brought things fairly up to date. And, as I said at the beginning, I am going to answer *all* my letters more promptly during this year. It is my only New Year *Resolution*. I hope 1933 will be *livable* for us all. That seems almost all one *dare* hope just now.

Yours faithfully
L. M. Macdonald

.

The Manse
Norval, Ont.

Oct 25/33

Dear Mr. MacMillan:

I can see the sarcastic and condescending smile with which you regard the date at the head of this letter. "She made a New Resolution to answer all personal letters within six weeks of their receipt!!!!" says that smile.

Mea culpa! I really have tried! But such a summer! And—your letter came on June 10th. A little over four

months ago! Isn't that really an improvement? I am sure
it is many years since I got around to it in four months.
But even so it was in January I wrote last and that is
"some stretch" to cover. So I must get me down to it
without further excuses. For a miracle I am alone to-
night and for a greater miracle I haven't got to go to a
social or a guild or a play practice. So I shall at least get a
letter begun. "Lucky" is purring on the table beside me
and watching me with bright round eyes. How dreadful
it would be *not* to love a cat! How much one would miss
out of life.

We have passed through a summer which, for terrible
and long continued heat and drouth, has not been
known in Ontario for over fifty years. Now that we *have*
passed through it, it seems like an incredible nightmare.
And yet one fortnight of it was the most delightful I
have known for years. My maid went away for her holidays and my friend Nora Campbell—she was Nora Lefurgey[1] thirty years ago and we were girls together and
sworn chums in old P.E.I.—came out and spent it with
me. And every night we went on a voyage to some magic
shore beyond the world's rim.

We did all the work together in the day time—and
such fun as we had. We joked—and talked beautiful
nonsense—and did things just for the fun of doing
them—and tried dozens of new recipes. And laughed!
Oh, how we laughed—such laughter as I have long been
a stranger to. I really thought I had forgotten how to
laugh like that.

And every evening after the supper dishes were finished, we walked *four miles* in a lovely ecstatic freedom
under a harvest moon up a lonely "back road" which
was not infested by cars. I hadn't believed there was anything like those walks left on earth. From the moment

1. Nora LeFurgey, born in St. Eleanors, Prince Edward Island, married Edmund E. Campbell and lived in Toronto. L.M. dedicated
Magic for Marigold to her.

164

we found ourselves amid the moon patterned shadows of that road every particle of our middle aged care and worry seemed to be wiped out of our minds and souls as if by magic. Hope was our friend again and we were no longer afraid of tomorrow. We just loitered on and on, through the faint enchanted moon fire, under the old old stars that had looked down on our girlhood rambles by a far-off sea. In daytime that road is quite commonplace but when steeped in moonlight it is magical. The trees along it seemed to stand in an exquisite silver hush and beyond it beauty seemed shimmering over the fields. The air was full of cricket song. The far hills and valleys were compact of some mystery and charm as old as time.

Sometimes we talked. Sometimes we merely walked in silence, tasting our own wild joy. When we did talk we said whatever came into our heads. We discussed every subject on earth from the lightest to the most profound. When we exhausted earth we adventured the heavens, to the remotest secrets of "island universes." Sometimes we quoted poetry. Nora would voice the first line of a couplet and I would finish it. Once in this alternate way we recited the whole of Wordsworth's Ode On the Intimations of Immortality, lingering over the lines "Our birth is but a sleep and a forgetting etc." Of course you know them. Our minds seemed to strike sparks from each other. It was *easy* to be witty and brilliant. We opened doors of memory long closed. We looked again on faded joys and dim old griefs that had once been agonies. Once we stopped beside a field gate and stood there in absolute silence for a whole hour uttering not a word, in a kind of divine trance, drinking in the loveliness of a sunset sky of rose and dark gold against which trees shaped themselves in eternal repose. And we were perfectly happy in our perfect indescribable communion with some great Over-Spirit which seemed to take complete possession of us.

And the moonlight views along the Credit! One night we walked along the river bank and came to a place so breath taking in its beauty that we sat on a tree trunk for over two hours and just looked at it. We hardly spoke in all those two hours. Never had I felt so close to the Soul of all beauty—so one with it. When we had to drag ourselves away we both felt that we had captured one of those things even time cannot destroy. And then on the way home we had what was simply the funniest adventure I ever had in my life. I can't narrate it for it would take hours, but when it was over Nora and I simply *reeled* home, drunken with laughter. In "life's unlit December"—if we ever come to it—we will recall it and see two jolly ghosts laughing under the moon. (Just at this point of writing a *green fly* alighted on my hand. I paused to examine it. It was about half an inch long and so incredibly slender that it reminded me of the old geometrical definition "length without breadth." And yet it was just as incredibly beautiful. The most exquisite pale green with a tiny, intricate, enamelled pattern in white along the back. I never saw anything like it before. What Power fashioned that tiny thing so perfectly and wasted (?) on it so much beauty and skill? No eye but mine ever saw or will see and appreciate it. To what end was it made so lovely? And why has the power that made it so made so many hideous human beings and so many bitter and ugly human lives?)

· · ·

What a pity the only authentic picture of Queen Mary was destroyed in that 1800 fire. However, I suppose some engraving of it is extant. I wonder which one it was. I have seen several pictures of Mary, none of which at all resemble the other, and, in spite of the fact that she was reputed to be a great beauty, not one of them seemed to my eyes even tolerably good-looking. If any

166

was authentic she must have owed her reputation to coloring and personal magnetism. This reminds me— years ago a travelling lecturer spoke in Cavendish hall and showed "magic lantern" views, among them a picture of the fair and fatal queen. Everyone in the audience gave an ejaculation of surprise. "Why, it is the image of Maud Montgomery," they said. I was not present and I do not know which of her so-called pictures it was. As I have just said, I do not think any picture I have seen at all beautiful, so I am not to be accused of vanity in repeating this yarn! And certainly I have never seen any resemblance to myself in any of them. Neither do I claim to be possessed by her spirit, like the lady in your clipping!

I am sure the arranging, or rather re-arranging of your books gave you great pleasure. It's wonderful to have them all together. *Our* books are scattered all over the house for the little room we call the library is not big enough for half of them. It has been always one of my dreams to have a real library with built-in shelves all around the walls. But in a manse one can never realize such a dream. When a house isn't your own you have to take it "as is" and make the best of it.

．　　．　　．

My boys are both in college now. Stuart is in his first year of medicine. At the Canadian National Exhibition this year he carried off the gold medal for gymnastics and so became junior champion of all Canada at the age of 17. I thought I had sent you one of his pictures in gym costume but I don't find your name on my list so I will enclose one to make sure. If you already have one you may return it.

My new book "Pat of Silver Bush" came out in September. I put your name on the list I sent to my Canadian publishers. Did you receive your copy? Some

167

whose names I sent in did not and I have been afraid
yours may have gone agley also. It has been very favorably reviewed. I really put more of *myself* into *Pat* than
into any other of my heroines.

· · ·

When this letter reaches you there will be a tang of good
wishes for Xmas in the air, so I enclose an advance of
them in this.

Yours fraternally,
L. M. Macdonald

INSTALMENT ONE

The Manse
Norval, Ont
Can.

Jan 22/35

Dear Mr. MacMillan:

· · ·

Last winter was a very severe winter in Canada—the
most severe for 85 years. The roads were *terrible* the
whole time. Snow would come—then rain would thaw
the snow to ice—then freeze. As a result all the roads
around here except the highways were coated with ice
and motoring on them was a terrible nervous strain. Mr.
Macdonald and I had to be out on them almost every
night and we got rather run down in every way. Then in
March, after a rather terrible experience one night in a
wild storm on an icy road and consequent exposure he
took a very bad attack of flu and after it was over he

began to have terrible and almost constant pain in the head. The doctors said it was nerves but they could not relieve it in any way. He could not sleep night after night and in May he broke down completely with nervous prostration. He could not sleep or study and his nerves were in a dreadful state. The doctors advised rest and he did not do anything until the middle of June. Then, I realizing that he was getting worse all the time, persuaded him to go to the Homewood Sanitarium at Guelph for treatment. For the first three weeks he was there he got worse instead of better and the constant pain in his head and continued insomnia except when taking a drug nearly drove him crazy. Then they did what they should have done in the first place—gave him a thorough physical examination. And they discovered that the whole of the lower bowel was impacted with fecal matter and must, the doctors said, have been like that for weeks and perhaps months. The poison was going through his system and producing the neuritis. They had a pretty difficult time getting it cleared up but they succeeded. In a week's time he began to improve rapidly and by mid August he came home, feeling fine and hoping to return to work in a couple of weeks. I asked the doctor what should be done to prevent any occurrence of the condition and he said to give him a table spoon of a certain "petrolager"—a laxative oil—every morning and a "blue pill" twice a week. I don't know if the term "blue pill" is known in Scotland but it is an old liver pill—not a potent affair and not "blue." The druggists make it up as required from "blue mass" and coat it with sugar or gelatine or anything that comes handy. On our way home from Guelph we called in at a Georgetown drug store and I asked the clerk for a box of "blue pills." He said they did not have any made up and it would take some time to prepare them, but he would run across to the drug store over the street and see if they had any ready. He came back with a small cardboard box marked in pencil "Blue Pills" and I brought them home. Next morning I first—thank heaven—gave Mr. M. the spoonful of petrolager and then I handed him a "blue pill"—a small bluish gray tablet. He took it and at once said it tasted "bitter," and when it was down he at once complained of a "burning sensation." I went at once to the phone. I was not alarmed but I thought a blue pill shouldn't act that way because I used to take them and they were quite "sensationless" in every way. I thought there was some mistake, so I rang up Mr. Robb and asked him if he was sure his clerk had given me blue pills. He said he "thought so." I said I did not think they were blue pills and that I would like him to go across to the other store and see just what they were. He promised to do so in a bored tone which seemed to imply, "Here is a crazy woman who must be humored." I went up to our room and found Mr. M. vomiting very freely. After he had finished he said he felt much better and asked me to run down to the P.O. and get the morning paper. I was gone about ten minutes only but when I returned Dr. Paul's car was at the gate. In alarm I ran up to the room. I shall never forget that dreadful sight. Mr. M. lay on the bed unconscious and looking like death—I thought he *was* dead, while Dr. Paul with his coat off and his sleeve rolled up, was jabbing a hypodermic in his arm.

At the moment I could not imagine what had happened but found out later on. When Mr. Robb investigated he found that what the clerk in the other store had given his clerk was the *deadliest bug-killer* on the market, composed of strychnine, bi-chloride of mercury and nicotene!!! Half a tablet was a fatal dose, and Mr. M. had taken a whole one! I fancy Mr. Robb's bored manner disappeared rather promptly. He phoned to Dr. Paul "For God's sake get up to Norval manse as quickly as you can." Dr. Paul reached up and snatched a bottle from his office shelf—an antidote to those very

poisons which had sat there *unopened* for twenty years!
He said afterwards if it had not been there he could
never have got it in time. He got here just in time to
force a dose of it down Mr. M's throat before the latter
collapsed from shock.

I, knowing nothing of this, gasped out, "Doctor, is he
dead?" "I don't know," said Dr. Paul. "There is no pulse
beat. I have given him the strongest heart stimulant
known and we will know in fifteen minutes." But *twenty
five* minutes passed with no sign—they seemed to me
like a hundred years. *Then* the pulse came back—and in
half an hour he regained consciousness. To cut it short,
his life was spared. Four things, under Providence, had
saved him. The petrolager, which had coated the stom-
ach and prevented the bi-chloride from burning it, the
fact that he had taken a double dose which made him so
sick at once that he threw up a great deal of the poison,
my phoning so quickly, and the doctor's having the antidote!

Really, it was all one of those grotesque ghastly things
you read of in newspapers but never think of happening to yourself!

But although his life was spared, the terrible shock to
the system simply set his nerves back worse than ever.
His headaches and insomnia returned and for two
months he was most miserable, night and day. Then,
when I had almost given up in despair he began to improve. Sleep returned, his head grew better and finally
the last of November he was so much improved that I
persuaded him to go down to "the Island" for a visit. He
stayed down till New Years and came home so well that
he was able to take his services [words illegible] for the
first time since April. You can—or you *can't*—imagine
my relief and thankfulness. Of course he will have to be
careful and not overdo for some time yet—but I think if
no other horrible thing happens he will be quite himself
soon.

Of course, all these months have been a terrible strain on myself. I could not sleep when he couldn't and the autumn with its dreary darkening days was very hard. Besides, there was so much extra church work I had to see to, as we just had supply on Sunday. While Mr. M. was away on the Island I staged a little breakdown of my own and for six weeks could not sleep or eat or work. Then I began to pick up and am feeling much better now. It is such a blessing that we are both able to sleep again! It really seems to be heaven to climb into bed every night and drift off into a sound slumber. From the first of May until the first of January I don't think I had *one* real sleep and nights on end I couldn't sleep any. So, in view of all this, you don't wonder, I'm sure, that letter writing was simply not on the map as far as I was concerned. I have had some hard years in my life but 1934 was by far the most ghastly I have ever lived through and I know life can never be quite the same again for either of us. We will never, I fear, *completely* recover from its strain and anxiety.

I am aghast, in referring to my notebook, that my last letter to you seems to have been written Nov 33. I knew it was a long time but I really thought I had written last winter. However I see the first of the pile of letters from you on my desk is dated Jan, 34 so I suppose I could not have done so. Well, I'll take these letters now and answer them but as I cannot write any more to-night—"tis the middle of the night by the castle clock"—and as I don't know just how soon I can "resume and continue" I am going to pop this into an envelope and send it to you at once. The other instalments will follow in due course—I hope!

Yours to be continued in the next
L. M. Macdonald

"Journey's End"

(letters from 1936 to 1941)

In 1935 the Macdonalds retire from Norval, and in April of
that year they move to a new house in the Swansea area of
Toronto. They call the house, appropriately, "Journey's End."
For L. M. Montgomery, the highlight of that first year, and in-
deed of all the Toronto years, is the receiving of the Order of the
British Empire from the Governor General of Canada.

The tone of the correspondence is melancholy. In the few letters written during these years, she is preoccupied with Ewen's
illnesses, which eventually lead to his complete mental and
physical breakdown. She is heartbroken by the death of her cat,
Lucky, and tells MacMillan: "Nothing in my life, except the
death of one dear friend [Frede Campbell], has caused me more
grief and loneliness." Her own health fails.

Nevertheless, she continues to write. To satisfy "pleading
publishers" she publishes Anne of Windy Poplars in 1936
and Anne of Ingleside in 1939. To satisfy herself she publishes Jane of Lantern Hill (dedicated to Lucky) in 1937,
telling MacMillan that she wrote it because she "loved it and its
little heroine. . . ."

She makes only two visits to Prince Edward Island during
these years, one in 1936 and the last in 1939. In the first visit
she has to become reconciled to the National Park in Cavendish, and her final visit is overshadowed by the outbreak of
World War II.

The last letter, written on December 23, 1941, is the most
touching of the whole correspondence.

173

> *210A* Riverside Drive
> Toronto, Ont.
> "Journey's End"

March 1/36

.　　.　　.

My notebook tells me that my last letter to you was written last winter somewhere around Feb. 1st. It seemed to me I had written you since then (apart from my note telling you of our moving to Toronto) but probably not. Mr. Macdonald found that he could not carry on with the heavy work of a country charge. So he resigned and we came to Toronto. All else will emerge in its proper place. (I write letters with my daily notebook on my desk and like to follow along day by day. This, of course, results in a sort of crazy patchwork epistle, but perhaps there is really more interest in it than if it were written on the classical models.)

Both Mr. M. and myself are feeling so much better than last spring. A good night's sleep is no longer the rarity it was during the two years preceding our coming to Toronto. And even in my wakeful hours I can see such beauty as I lie in bed as almost reconciles me to wakefulness. For I pull up all the shades on the large triple window before I go to bed and then I can see the great pine tops tossing against the sky—with the moon behind them if there is a moon—and the lights along the lake shore twinkling like jewels on the dark bosom of the night.

We have called our new home "Journey's End" and I hope it is the end of our wanderings. I have packed and moved three times and I hope never again. It is truly what somebody has called a "Herculaneum" task, especially when one has as many books as we have. Of course this moving was not quite so hard as our previous ones, for we had a moving van at the last. But almost everything had to be packed first—at least all dishes, pictures, and books etc.—then unpacked and placed, and it was all really very very hard work, especially so coming at the end of a year of strain and anxiety.

We had a dreary time at first trying to get a house in Toronto and haunting agencies. There is an acute shortage of houses in Toronto and nothing we could get for what we could afford to pay in rent suited us at all. Finally we decided to buy, as the interest on a mortgage would not be much more than half what we would pay in rent. We were lucky enough to get a nice brand new house in the Swansea suburb. It is not really in Toronto, save geographically. We have our own municipal government and it is all really just like a nice country village where everybody knows everybody else. We live on a winding road on the bank of the Humber River. Around us are nice homes with nice gardens and lots of *breathing space* and behind us is a deep ravine of pines and oaks. In summer the ravine is carpeted with bracken ferns and all kinds of dainty wild flowers grow there. Ever since we came to Norval when we came into Toronto our road led right through here and I used to say "When we retire I'd like to live here," but I really never dared hope we would. That is one "dream come true" anyhow. And it is very delightful to *own* one's home and feel free to do just as one pleases in and about it. In a manse, no matter how nice it may be, you never feel this. Next month—next year—you may be leaving it and going elsewhere. One never has a sense of *permanency*. And our house being new is very convenient. We have two fireplaces, three bathrooms and all kinds of electrical "plugs" for sweeping, ironing and washing etc. Housework is really a pleasure. And we have the boys with us again, which has not been the case for many years.

．　　　．　　　．

175

In June, as I wrote you, the King gave his "trusty and well-beloved Lucy Maud Montgomery Macdonald" the O.B.E. (I wonder if the poor man ever heard of me before he signed the warrant!) In September I went to Ottawa and was "invested." The function was rather quiet, owing to their being in mourning for the Queen of Belgium, but it was very interesting, especially when the Knights were "dubbed." The insignia of the O.B.E. is a large very handsome gold Maltese cross with the King's monogram on it, attached to a bow of the royal purple ribbon. We can wear it only when a representative of the King is present, but can have a miniature of it made which may be worn to evening affairs.

And poor King George is gone! It all seems rather unbelievable. His death seemed to affect us in Canada much more *personally* than either King Edward's or Queen Victoria's—perhaps because having heard him so often over the radio we really felt as if we knew him. I wonder what sort of a King Edward the 8th will be. Isn't it odd that there is King but no Queen? I doubt if he will ever marry now. If not I believe there will be another "Queen Elizabeth" one day. I found the pictures in the papers you sent very interesting. We "listened" to the funeral service "on the air" and today we heard King Edward's first official speech to his Empire. I never cease to marvel over the radio. It does seem like witchcraft and I suppose the people who "hear" will also "see" in twenty more years.

We brought our two pussy cats with us—"Good Luck" and "Pat." They did not seem to mind the change at all. They settled down right away on their own cushions and seemed quite happy and contented from the start. But alas, in July dear old Paddy died. He took sick suddenly one day—we found him lying paralyzed from "the waist" down. The vet said it was gastritis but I think it was just old age. He was fifteen years old. Still, he had been quite smart right up to then and had all his teeth.

When he died everyone in the family cried. When you've had a pet for 15 years he is *one* of the family. When he came my boys were five and eight and now they are young men. He was never an affectionate cat— never wanted petting and was very snarly and growly. But he was handsome and *always round*. We missed him at every turn. We buried him under the oaks of the ravine and his memory will long be green in our annals. Luck missed him. Luck too is growing old—how I hate to admit it. He will be 13 this spring. But he is still beautiful and loving. Ah me, these little creatures take too much out of our lives when they go—not only their sleek furry bodies but somehow all the years they spent with us, and leave a terrible hole.

I hope you received the copy of "Mistress Pat" I had sent you. I have just finished and handed over to the publishers a new *Anne* book—"Anne of Windy Poplars."!! My publishers were most anxious for me to write it—they thought it would be a good commercial venture after the film.[1] So very unwillingly I agreed. At first I thought I could never "get back" into that series. It seemed to belong to another world. But after the plunge I began to find it possible—nay to enjoy it—as if I really had found my way back to those golden years before the world went mad. I wrote a story of the three years between "Anne of the Island" and "Anne's House of Dreams" when she was teaching in Summerside. I don't know whether I have succeeded in recapturing the old spirit and atmosphere or not, even in part. I shall await your verdict on that point with much interest. The book will be out next fall. I wrote it in five months—a stunt that I have not done since I wrote "Green Gables." Of course I have more time for writing now, but even so it was a rather breathless performance. It is my 19th book!!

⋅ ⋅ ⋅

1. *Anne of Green Gables* was made into a silent film in 1921 and into a "talkie" in 1934.

So, my dear friend, another letter closes. As we grow older we wonder—"how many more." But I shan't close on a sorrowful note. No, it is better to think of all those island universes we have yet to explore!

Yours sincerely,
L. M. Montgomery Macdonald

"Journey's End"
210A Riverside Drive
Toronto, Ont.

December 27, 1936

Dear Mr. MacMillan:
This is really breaking the record with a vengeance. Here am I writing—or at least beginning—the *second* letter to you in the same year. My first was dated March 16 and this one is four days before 1937. What does such a portent foretell? Well, I think nothing much more amazing will happen in '37 than has happened in '36.

Ex King Edward and Mrs. Simpson!!!!!!!

However, to glance over your letters again and answer them first. I shall not of course finish this at one sitting. It will very likely drag over into the next year. But when a letter is once *begun* I always feel that it is off my conscience. Though I don't like that phrase. It sounds as if one were doing something because one *ought*— some unpleasant duty or penance. Such an idea is of course utterly at variance with the truth. I enjoy writing letters to you quite as much as receiving them. It is only that I *don't* like writing them piecemeal, now a little and then a little. But as yet it seems the only way. I so rarely have an undisturbed half hour.

The first thing to be dealt with is "Instalment 2," begun in November 1935 and finished in April 1936— consequently not received by me in time to be discussed in my letter of March. I don't know how it is with you but I enjoy discussing your news and opinions quite as much and indeed more than relating my news and opinions. And the first thing in that instalment is your opinion of the Anne picture, which I enjoyed very much—I mean your opinion, not the picture—though of course I enjoyed that too.

Seven times! I saw it only four. Yes, I think "Anne Shirley" was a very good Anne, all things considered, lacking some of what I tried to convey as a certain delicate elfin charm. Her *eyes* were good and in the scene where she "floated down to Camelot" she *was* Anne completely and satisfyingly. Despite the newspaper I consider her beautiful, though not with the sugary prettiness of so many "film" stars. She and I correspond occasionally. And it does give me the oddest thrill to be walking along a Toronto street and suddenly see a neon sign flaming out "Anne Shirley in So-and-So." I have the weirdest sensation that *Anne* has really come to life.

I forget if I told you *my* reactions to the characters too. Probably I did. I agree with you in all your statements, except one. Helen Westley would have been *perfect* as Mrs. Lynde. Why they blended Mrs. Barry and Mrs. Lynde is "one of thoth thingth no fellow can underthtand." But I *don't* think as you do that Gertrude Messenger was a good Diana. She was too fair and babyish. *My* Diana was a dark lady with sloe-black hair and flashing black eyes. I didn't like *Gilbert at all* and I haven't come across anybody who did. So you certainly are "with the multitude." The indignant letters I've got from girls about it!!

As for the scenery *two* scenes in the picture were photographed on the Island. One was the opening one and the other was the *background* of the scene where Anne is talking to Matthew while he was fencing. All the rest is *pure California.* The house shown, both interior and exterior is no house in P. E. Island, and does not resemble any farmhouse with which I am acquainted. The real house they photographed is somewhere in California. Mr. Webb,[1] who is married to a cousin of mine, lives in a house on the farm where *Lover's Lane* is and this place is often referred to as *Green Gables* though in reality *Green Gables* was practically imaginary. As for the snap that you enclose it is not my old home but a picture of the old *Cavendish manse,* now superseded by a new one. I can't imagine why I ever sent it to you, unless it was because it was taken very soon after I got my first camera and was proudly sending out any thing I took right and left. I must have sent you a snap of my old home sometime. I'll get one printed off some of these days and send it—I have the original plate by me yet.

. . .

Thanks for the clipping from the Newsagent containing its comment on the Daily Mirror's choice of Anne as the romantic book of the month. In regard to the "bits" it quotes from Anne, here is an amusing chit. I sent one MS. of the story to Harraps and one to Stokes, my N.Y. publishers. The Stokes readers thought that some of the incidents mentioned in Anne's walk through the churchyard and later on in her visit to "Tomgallon House" were "too gruesome" and advised they be cut out. So accordingly I cut. Always before the English editions were printed from the U.S. plates and so I supposed this book would be, too, and did not think it necessary to tell the Harraps about it. But for the first time they made their own plates. So all these "gruesome things" are in the English edition and nobody seems to have suffered. But the joke is that one of these bits is quoted in the Newsagent's article as being one of the amusing things in the book!!!

My own title was "Anne of Windy Willows." But

1. Ernest Webb (1880-1950), married Myrtle Macneill (1883-1969) in 1905.

Stokes thought this title too reminiscent of Kenneth Grahame's fairy animal story "The Wind In The Willows" (you sent me this book one Xmas and I've re-read it a score of times and enjoy every reading of it more than the last). I thought this very far-fetched but suggested "Poplars" in place of "Willows." But Harraps scouted the idea and insisted on retaining "Willows." Mr. Harrap said the English people knew very little about poplars and all about willows!! So there you are.

     .   .   .

The last of September I went down to P. E. Island and spent October there. I had not been down for *four* years—the longest time I had ever spent away from it. As I went in the autumn I saw all the gorgeous autumn coloring again. And I saw many many old friends. And alas, there were some I did not see nor will ever see again in this life. There is always this sorrow now about "going back home." In the churches I seemed to know so few—so few. New generations have grown up of which I know nothing. The *grand*children of people at whose weddings I danced are big boys and girls now. But my woods and shore were the same and there were still enough old friends to have a royal good time with. All the chicken dinners I ate!!

And all the old beauty. I had forgotten that the ponds and rivers of P. E. Island were so brilliantly, so unbelievably blue. I walked and prowled by night and day as I have not done for years.

But I found Cavendish, or part of it, in the shadow of a great oncoming change—a change that at first made me feel heartbroken but which I have now come to see will really be for the best in the long run. A few words of explanation must come here. When I was a girl on the old Cavendish farm I loved it very much. But there were no woods on it. It was all under cultivation though there were plenty of trees scattered here and there and an embracing grove of spruce and maple and birch around the house itself. So I had to seek other farms for woods. Just across the road from us was a block of three farms. The center one belonged to my mother's cousin David Macneill. At the back of the farm was a large belt of woodland which was my favorite haven. Lover's Lane was there and the Birch Path and the "Haunted Wood" and the brook below Green Gables and the Dryad's Bubble. As a child I almost lived in these woods. As a girl I roamed there every evening and "thought" out the stories I would write next day.

David Macneill was an old bachelor and lived with his sister Margaret. I used to wonder worriedly what would happen when he died—into whose hands the farm would fall. I feared it would be someone who would not care for beauty or the old traditions—someone who might even cut down the woods. My fears turned out to be groundless. David and Margaret adopted an orphan niece, Myrtle Macneill who became an intimate friend of mine. She eventually married a very fine man, Ernest Webb, and he just stepped in and hung up his hat. They both loved the place and were careful to preserve all its beauty spots. For twenty five years, whenever I went back to the Island I have made my headquarters there. My own old home had been torn down and the Webb place became my second home. I was "Aunt Maud" to the Webb children and we made the old house ring with laughter.

Things did not go quite so well with the farms on the other side. One of them belonged to a certain Pierce Macneill who had no family. When he died the farm was bought for pasture land by a man who did not live there and has been going rapidly down for the past few years. The back fields all "went spruce"—you couldn't believe how incredibly quick a farm can grow up with spruce on P. E. Island when it ceases to be cultivated. On the other side was a farm owned by Hamilton Macneill (Cavendish was the habitat of the clan Macneill. My mother was a Macneill.) It contained the pond which the Cavendish people persist in calling the Lake of Shining Waters. Hamilton is an old bachelor and when he would die the farm would be in the market. As it was a very small though a good one and as Pierce Macneill's farm was sold out I have always been in terror that some French Canadian (of whom there are quite a large number on the Island) would buy them, as they like to do in the case of worn-out farms.

Now, the Dominion Gov't is giving a *National Park* to every Province. And they decided that the place for the P.E.I. Park was Cavendish, because it was already a sort of shrine on account of my books and because it had a magnificent sand beach and was situated between two beautiful harbors—Rustico and New London Harbors (the latter being "Four Winds"). And, because of the Anne books they decided to buy these farms for the park, as they run out to the sandshore.

At first, as aforesaid, I felt very badly. The old Webb house and barns would have to go and much change would come. But when I found out that Mr. Webb was to remain as a caretaker of the Park, I felt reconciled. The Premier[2] assured me that the woods and paths and dykes would be kept just as they were etc. So I began to feel that it was all for the best because those places will never be desecrated now. Still, there will be a good deal of change and I felt very very sad my last night there. For it would be my last night in that old house where we have had so many happy hours. The Gov't is going to build a new house for the Webbs and no doubt it will be a very nice one *but it will not be the same.*

The brook and pond are in the park, too, and the old site of the school I went to. Really, when I first penned Anne of Green Gables so many years ago I had no idea what would spring from it all. The Gov't is going to

2. Thane A. Campbell, Premier of the Island from 1936-1943.

183

build a highway along the shore, connecting the two harbors.

"Change and decay in all around I see"—well, perhaps it is not exactly "decay" in this case but how we do hate to see any kind of change, even change for the better, as we grow older.

I suppose I can't close this letter without saying something about the Ex-King!!!

Hasn't it all been terrible? To think that a man would throw away the crown of the greatest empire of the world because of his infatuation for a middle-aged divorcee with two living husbands! It is almost unbelievable. If he had been a boy in his twenties one could have understood it. If Mrs. Simpson had been a woman of unblemished reputation I believe the majority of his people would have said, "Let him marry her." But as it was it was too rank. I fear he will live to repent what he has done, when he awakens from his dream to find himself a man without a career and without a country—and without real love. For, had Mrs. Simpson really loved him, she would have removed herself out of his life long ago and would never have allowed him to ruin himself for her. I shall be much interested in hearing of your reaction to the affair. I think Baldwin handled the crisis marvellously. Something terrible might so easily have come of it if there had been the slightest false step.

Well, we have lived in strange times—no stranger in all history I verily believe. Since 1914 the world has been a nightmare. Sanity seems to have departed from it.

May 1937 bring you many many happy days. The wish is old but ever new and sincere. I shall hope for a letter from you before very long. I began this letter in 1936 but as I foresaw did not finish it. It is now Jan. 11, 1937. Even the century is beginning to get mature. Soon it will be middle aged.

Yours fraternally
L. M. Macdonald

"Journey's End"
210A Riverside Drive
Toronto, Ont.

Feb. 23/38

Dear Mr. MacMillan:
I'm going to begin a letter to-night at least.

I think in all our correspondence I have as a rule writ-ten *cheerful* letters, have I not! My life has had its share—sometimes I am tempted as now to feel *more* than its share of worries and trials and sorrows. But I haven't really said much about them in my letters, have I? Well, I'm afraid I'm going to break my record. I am afraid that this letter, no matter how much I shall as-suredly try to make it what I would like it to be, will *not* be a very cheerful or inspirational epistle. For over a year now my life has been one of worry and strain and anxiety, some of which can be told, some of which can-not. As a result I have rather broken down. The last eight years have all been *very* hard in many ways and this one coming on the top of them all—well, I just haven't been able to stand up to it quite. I don't eat or sleep or feel much interest in anything; and worst of all I can see no likely end to this—no time when I can say "It will be over by then"—"after that I can pick life up and go on." And so I'm in rather bad shape and am not quite able to hide it, as I have often hidden it in the past when I was worried and anxious, writing letters, sometimes that may have *read* quite brightly, in spite of their back-ground.

·   ·   ·

The first envelope of yours I open contains your Xmas card and a note of good wishes. I do think a Christmas card bearing the sender's photograph is always the very nicest kind of a card. I should judge it good of you, too.

185

And how literary you do look. My own picture on the wall does come out surprisingly well. I always rather liked that picture. I am going to put the card for a bookmark in the book you sent. *It* did "ring the bell." I enjoyed it *very very* much. I forget if I sent a note with the book I sent you "The Country Kitchen." I liked it because the life it painted was in so many respects exactly like my own in the old P. E. Island farmhouse of long years ago. It may not appeal to you at all. But at least it will give you a very clear picture of life, even to-day, in our American and Canadian farmhouse. And I liked the humor in it, too.

In the same envelope were three "Something I want to say" clippings and your Bank Street Ballad—which was very amusing. Some lights do make people look ghastly. The clipping on "Home" brought the tears to my eyes. Somehow this past year I have often felt very homesick for my own "Island." There *is* something about an Island that isn't found in any other spot—some nameless magic—some indefinable charm.

· · ·

Your reactions to the Anne books were very interesting and your criticisms entirely just. But it isn't always easy to spin books wholly "out of my own personality" and sometimes I just have to fall back on my notebook to make the book long enough. In my latest book "Jane of Lantern Hill"—I sent you a copy—I think I was not guilty of this fault. I wrote the book because I loved it and its little heroine and I think the only chapter you won't find in keeping is the one about Jane and the lion. And yet something very like that did happen somewhere in the Maritimes years ago. Only in the real case the lion *followed* the lady who was considerably older!

I have now commented on the outstanding passages in your letter. And having got so far will go to bed, for my head is beginning to ache a bit. I am not sleeping

186

very well of late and so I do not keep late hours of work. I shall "resoom and continue" as soon as possible.

The first dreadful happening in 1937 was the death of my darling pussy cat, who died on the evening of January 18th.

Nothing in my life, except the death of one dear friend, has caused me more grief and loneliness. Even today more than a year later I cannot bear to think of it. I missed—and miss—him heartbreakingly in every detail of life. There is rarely a night that, waking, the tears do not come into my eyes when I realize I cannot put out my hand and feel his silken flank in the darkness somewhere on my bed. Lucky was thirteen and a half years old. For the greater part of five thousand nights and days he had been my inseparable companion. And such a companion! When an ordinary cat dies you are grieved. But you know there are plenty more cats like him in the world. Luck was unique. He had every virtue a cat could have and not a single fault. He was beautiful, affectionate, graceful, intelligent—so intelligent that you felt he was human. He was the only *perfect* thing I have ever seen in this world. Well, never did a cat have a happier life than Luck. Never was there an animal so full of the "joy of living." He loved to be petted, praised, caressed. He could not bear to be ignored or neglected. If he felt himself so he would retreat under the side board, like an Adulamite to his cave, and sit there, looking at you with the most reproachful eyes until you called him out and made amends.

He always ran to meet me when I came home. He was more like a dog than a cat in this respect. He had his own favorite nooks and corners all over the house, and I cannot bear to look at them. But he spent part of every night on my bed, and always while I wrote he had to be somewhere near.

I knew Lucky was growing old but I did not *really* believe he would ever die. He was one of those vital creatures of whom, when they die, we feel it is impossible to believe they are dead. Even yet I think of it with a sort of desperate incredulity. How could that beauty, grace, charm, affection pass into nothingness.

Lucky died of cancer of the liver. He never suffered any pain—just grew weaker and weaker day by day as his appetite failed. He kept up all his dear habits and engaging ways to the last. He simply starved to death, although I gave him cod liver oil capsules every day. He was always such a darling about taking medicine. And every time I touched him he purred. Only in the last twelve hours he ceased to purr. He was too far away by that time on a road where he could have no companion—not even I who had loved him so much.

His vitality was amazing. I am sure if that horrible thing had not fastened on him he would have lived for years yet.

He passed his last day lying on my bed. I watched by him all day, keeping him warmly covered—but I could not keep away the steadily creeping chill of death.

Then—the little gray flank heaved no more. I thought he was dead. I put my hand on his head. Breathing had ceased but at my touch he suddenly opened his mouth in a tiny soundless meow. His last moment of life was literally a response to my touch. It was as if he said, "Yes, I still know and love you—I must still respond to your caress." We buried him the next day on the edge of the rock garden by a little pine tree.

From my earliest recollection a certain stone sat at the corner of the apple orchard at my old Cavendish home. Where it had come from I never knew. It was some kind of gray granite, with no affinity with Island stone which is red sandstone. Likely someone once brought it up from the shore. It may have been part of the ballast of some vessel. It was almost perfectly round—a huge ball about 4 feet in circumference. Grandmother always used it as a weight for her cheese press (she was noted for her cheese. All cheese made in those days was "home made.") The lads who came in the evenings for their mail tied their nags to the orchard fence and when they mounted them again used the old stone as a "leaping stone." Many a summer evening I sat on it to learn my lessons—there was a tall old spruce tree growing over it then—and many an autumn evening I sat on it while the "pigs potatoes" were boiled in the huge round iron boiler and the sparks streamed to the stars when the fire under it was poked.

The last time I was on the Island I made my usual pilgrimage to the old home site—alas it grows more jungle like every year—and I found the old stone still there at the corner of the almost vanished orchard. It was almost buried in the earth, only its top showing. Two falls ago I wrote to my cousin and asked him if he would let me have the old stone. He dug it up, crated it, and shipped it to me by freight. It arrived just before the New Year. I had meant to put it somewhere in my rock garden. Well, I put it on Lucky's grave. It seemed fitting. He was a P. E. Island cat and it became him to have a "stone" from the old sod.

"He was a cat—take him for all in all,
We shall not look upon his like again."

Last winter was for me one of bitter and ceaseless strain and worry. Worry over many things—some of them the kind that can't be told to the world but must be hidden and not spoken of. We all have such worries, no doubt, at some period of our lives, and find life very difficult while they last. There is no use in saying much about it.

Besides this Mr. Macdonald's health was very poor almost all the year. He had bronchitis all winter and developed a terrible cough which kept him awake at nights and so brought on one of his nervous breakdowns in the spring—quite the worst one of all that he has had. Indeed, it was more than nerves this time—for about two months in the summer he was a mental case and, among other symptoms, lost his memory completely. I could not bear to have him go to any institution for I knew no one could understand him as I did, for I have nursed him through so many of these attacks. But you can have some idea the stress and strain it meant. In August he began to recover and, as usual, recovered very quickly, so that by September he was able to go away to the Island for a visit. He was quite better when he returned but in November the cough and headaches returned and until about a month ago he was very miserable. Then he went to a new doctor and since then has been feeling much better. His cough has almost disappeared and he sleeps well and his nerves are much better. I do hope the improvement continues. He has had such a hard year.

· · ·

The summer, as I have said, was filled by Mr. Macdonald's serious illness. Then when he was better and had gone to the Island for his convalescence I came down with a very bad attack of acute sciatica. For six months I really had a terrible time. The pain was unbearable when I lay down so that I got very little sleep and my nerves, already strained, broke altogether. At the end of six weeks it left me as suddenly and reasonlessly as it had come. But I have been very nervous ever since and a prey to insomnia. Of course the latter is due to worry—of which I cannot write. It's just one of those things one must bear in silence and I mention it only that you may understand why I am rather broken down. I hope the clouds will pass some day and I shall regain in part at least, my old outlook on life.

By the way, did I ever send you a little magazine "The Maritime Advocate," containing an article of mine? I forget if I did or not. If not, just drop a card and I'll send you one. I'd rather like you to see the sketch.

I enclose a few clippings that may interest you. Don't you like Hardy's poem on his cat? I am sorry this letter is such a lifeless epistle. I hope my next one will be better, and I hope you can write soon. I think a letter from you would help me to regain a more normal outlook on life.

Yours sincerely,
L. M. Macdonald

"Journey's End"
210A Riverside Drive
Toronto, Ont.
Can.

March 7/39

Dear Mr. MacMillan:
It is with great satisfaction that I contemplate the foregoing address and date. It is such an achievement to *get started*. And it is not *quite* a year since my last letter to you. That was written on March *28*, 1938, so I am a few days to the good. And having begun I feel that I shall sometime make the finish. So, without further ado or apology I shall at once take up your letters and envelopes and proceed to answer them duly.

.   .   .

Judging by your second paragraph I mentioned something in my last letter about a failure in health. Well, I may as well say what there is to say on that subject and get rid of it.

I was not feeling well when I wrote and had not been for some months. For five years I have been under a ceaseless strain of worry of some kind or another and at last I crumpled. Soon after I wrote that letter I broke down altogether and for four months lived in a sort of hell on earth. My "nerves" went utterly. I could not sleep or work or sit still. I could only pace the floor. I would not live those four months over for anything that could be offered me. I will not write more of them. For certain reasons I could not go away from home so I had to fight it out here. In June I began to improve and I recovered with extraordinary rapidity—as one does sometimes in "nerves." Moreover, in August a bitter worry of more than two years standing was suddenly and unexpectedly removed. This, of course, greatly aided my recovery. I began to sleep—eat—*work*. Oh, the blessedness of being able to *work* again—to enjoy it! Truly, Elizabeth Barrett Browning was right when she said,

"For God in cursing gives us better gifts
Than men in benediction."

I know exactly what a soul, fished out of purgatory and wafted to heaven feels like!!!

I had better health up to New Year's than I have known for ten years. Then I ran into a strait of rough going—but not of a serious nature. The first week in January I was ill for a week and thought I had got through with my annual dose of "flu." Everyone in the household took it in turn and I nursed them all through it. Then ten days ago I came down again with a *dreadful* attack of flu. It has been sweeping over the whole of Canada like a scourge. Almost as bad as the terrible "Spanish flu" of 1918-19. But not so fatal. Almost all the victims have recovered but it has left us limp as rags and weak as water. Today I feel like the "wreck of old decency." But my "nerves" have not been affected and I hope to be all right again in a few weeks. The most racking cough goes with it and at times I cough till the tears pour from my eyes. It is over six years since I had such a bad attack. And I sincerely hope it will be twice that number before I have another!! Every one who has had it tells the same story of extraordinary prostration. If any doctor could discover, isolate, and find a serum for the "flu" germ he should be canonized and I would make a yearly pilgrimage to his shrine on my knees! Well, this disposes of my health. Apart from the "flu" I am again a "well woman" and besottedly thankful that I am.

I wish I could say the same of Mr. Macdonald. He was really quite well all summer and up to New Year's. But since then he has been very miserable. He suffers so from neuritis and bronchitis and of course damp and cold weather (of which we have had a great deal this winter) aggravate both complaints. He loses sleep and that affects his nerves adversely. I shall be doubly glad when spring comes. He is aways better when he can get out in the sunshine and take part at his beloved bowling club. He won first prize for the season last year.

． ． ．

March 12/39

Blessed are those who faint not for in due time they shall get their letters written. I have had a houseful of company these past ten days and haven't had a spare moment. Yesterday and to-day, too, are the first days I have felt like myself after the "flu."

I must thank you especially for the wonderful post cards of the Glasgow Exhibition you enclosed. They were beautiful and fascinating. Do you remember that it was at the Glasgow Exhibition we first met in person. Not long ago I came across an old snap shot I had taken of you and Ewan standing together in front of our edifice with a tall white tower. It seems "but the other day" and yet it is nearly 28 years ago and our whole world, as we knew it then, has passed away.

193

The "illuminations" must have been lovely. They do such wonderful things with coloured lights now. I think the post card which most intrigued me was the one showing the Victoria Falls in Rhodesia. (By the way *can* you tell me how that name is pronounced? I have never met anyone who could. Is it "Rhodes-sia"—or "Rhodeshia"—or something else again?) It has always been one of my desires to see the great "Victoria Nyanza." Of course the dream will never be fulfilled—in this incarnation, anyway.

The clipping "China dogs" interested me greatly. You will remember that I bought a pair of large lovely china dogs in York—or at least I think I wrote you about getting them. They were white with gold spots, with a "chain and padlock" around their necks, just as Lady Sackville describes. Ever since they have been presiding with dignity and aplomb at my fireside. They were 98 years old when I got them in a little shop huddled at the base of the mighty York minster, so they are nearly 126 now. I called them Gog and Magog. And in this connection we have two family jokes which are a bit funny. One day when Chester was about three a lady caller was in the living room and Chester gravely introduced them. "This is *God* and this is *My God*"!!

History repeated itself and Stuart in his turn essayed to inform a caller as to the dogs' names "This is Gog and this is *Aunt May's Gog*." (He has an Aunt May). I loved the "Woods" by Lady MacAllister. The "Moonlight" picture was very remarkable and beautiful.

Speaking of "photographs": you will likely remember that I was given a moving picture camera several years ago when I was a judge on an international kodak competition. We have had a great deal of pleasure and amusement out of it, though we cannot afford many films, they are so expensive. The other evening, being alone, I ran all the old films through the kodascope and

194

I don't know whether they gave me more pleasure or more pain. They were *ghostly*. Three dear friends of ours have died in the past three years—yet there they were, walking, laughing, talking, in those pictures. And there was *Lucky*, in picture after picture, walking proudly over the lawn, being petted and caressed— Lucky *alive*. I just couldn't stand it! For, two years after his death, it seems to me that I miss Lucky as much as ever—miss him at every turn. And there in one of those pictures I had him in my arms and he was rubbing his head against my face. You just can't imagine how it hurt me.

.   .   .

Do you know what gave me a positive thrill one day last fall? I got a letter from *Jerusalem* about *Jane of Lantern Hill*. Of course it was written by an Englishwoman living there. But when I thought of a book of mine being read in that city, "half as old as time," where David and Solomon reigned and the Great Teacher walked, I really cannot describe *how* I felt.

On September first I began work on a new book and finished it at New Years, "Anne of Ingleside." Yes, another Anne book, much against my will and in response to pleading publishers. However, it seems profitable to write Anne books. The R.K.O. Co. of Hollywood have within the last few days bought the *screen* rights to *Anne of Windy Willows*. This has been pleasantly exciting. Moreover, they want an option on "Anne's House of Dreams." I can't imagine how they'll make a picture out of Windy Willows ("Poplars" in America) because it is just a series of disconnected stories strung together on the thread of Anne's personality but no doubt they will inject a good deal of their own invention. "Anne of Ingleside" is really more about Anne's children than about her and I don't think it is "up to" the other books in the series.

And now for another co-incidence!! In order that you may understand it I must tell you a bit of family history. (I may have told it before, in which case skip it.)

Nearly two hundred years ago, in 1770 three Montgomery brothers and their wives set sail from Scotland for Quebec. It was a long and stormy voyage, even for those days, and poor Mary MacShannon Montgomery, wife of Hugh Montgomery was increasingly seasick from the time she left the shores of the old World until she came in sight of the new. In the gulf of St. Lawrence the vessel ran out of water and the captain decided to send a boat to the shore of P. E. Island (then St. John's Island, all woods, except for a few French and Indian settlements around the shore.) As it would take a day to stock up with *water* the captain told Mary Montgomery that she might go ashore with the crew and spend a day on dry land. (It is one of our family scandals that Mary M. bribed him to do it with a bottle of good Scotch whiskey!)

The moment Mary Montgomery's foot touched dry land she said, "Here I stay." (This may be familiar to you as I used the incident in "Emily of New Moon.") And there she did stay. In vain her husband pleaded. She vowed that never again as long as she lived would she set foot in any kind of vessel. Hugh had to land there too with all his goods and chattels, while his two brothers sailed on to Quebec.

Hugh took up land and cleared it, becoming the founder of the Montgomery family in P. E. Island, (starting it by a family of sixteen children). He was my great-great grandfather. As for the two brothers who went to Quebec, they might as well have gone to a different planet. In those days there was no communication between Upper Canada and the Maritimes. There is no record or legend that Hugh ever heard from or of them again. Even their names were not known to my generation nor could anybody ever tell me what they were.

Now, in my "talks" on my books and their background I have always told this tale, to account for my "good fortune" in being born in P. E. Island, instead of Quebec. I am sure I have told it a hundred times and never had any response or expected any. But one night in December I went out to Thornhill, a suburb of Toronto, to speak at the Annual Banquet of the World Horticultural Society. I told this story again. After the affair was over a Mrs. Colclough, wife of the Anglican rector at Thornhill came up to me and said, "I can tell you the names of the brothers who went on to Quebec. They were Richard and Alexander. My mother was a Montgomery, a great-great granddaughter of Richard!"

You can just imagine my delight and surprise. She said Alexander had not liked Canada and had gone back to Scotland. Richard did not stay in Quebec but came down to Ontario, settled near what was to be the city of Toronto and many of his descendants are still around here. His grandson was the "General Montgomery" who figured in the war of 1812 and "Montgomery's Tavern," famous in Ontario history was kept by another.

Mrs. Colclough said when I got up to speak she actually gave a jump, I was so remarkably like a cousin of hers. Another cousin, she said, has all the family history written out and I mean to get in touch with her and read it. There were several more interesting details into which time and space forbid my going. But I might mention one. I think I have told you that it was always a tradition in our family that we were originally descended from or connected with the Earls of Eglinton. My grandfather, Senator Montgomery, was said to be strikingly like the then earl and had been mistaken for him in London by the said earl's nephew. So ran the legend but to tell the truth I have often felt skeptical about it and thought the wish may just have been father to the thought. But Mrs. Colclough said it was quite true

197

and "Eglinton Avenue" one of the great trunk streets of Toronto was so named because the land was originally purchased by the city from a descendant of Richard who insisted that the new street be so named. With this confirmation I concede that it is probably true.

Now, don't you call that a Co-incidence with a capital?

March 24, 1939

Another whack at this letter which, to quote your own expression is more like a diary than a letter. Since I stopped with that last entry Hitler has *struck again*. He *must be stopped but how*?? I still cling to faith in my dream. But perhaps that Mighty Arm was the arm of *War* and it may come yet. Hitler is simply the head of a band of gangsters. (Did you know his *real* name was Shickelgruber?? Well, it is—or was. He had it changed by an Act of the Reich or something equivalent.)

We are, of course, all looking forward with mounting excitement to the visit of the King and Queen. I do hope nothing will occur to prevent it. They will spend only eight hours in Toronto, so I daresay we will hardly get a glimpse of them. The C.P.R. is getting out a memorial booklet[1] for them, illustrated with special oil paintings and I have been asked to write the chapter on P. E. Island. And now I think I have come to an end of my subject matter for this time. During the last two days spring has called. We have had ever since New Year's such a *nasty* winter of storms and cold. March has been a *mean* month. But these two days have made such a change and I do hope we are at an end of our cold weather and bad walking.

Yours faithfully
L. M. Montgomery Macdonald

1. *The Spirit of Canada.*

P.E.Island
September 23, 1939
[Postcard]

Am here for a month. Come for a walk with me on this shore tonight and we will forget for an hour the nightmare that has been loosed on the world. It is unfair that we should have to go through this *again*.

L. M. Macdonald

210A Riverside Drive
Toronto, Ont.

March 14/40

Dear Mr. MacMillan:

This isn't a letter but just a note to thank you for the book you sent at Xmas. I am so glad to have my "Flower Patch" set complete again. I've been waiting, thinking that letter you promised me way back in July when you returned from your vacation, might be along. I hope it wasn't written and sent—and sent down by a U-Boat. That you yourself are still doing business at the old stand is evident from the two packets of John O'Londons which came to hand a couple of days ago and were joyfully welcomed. Also the papers containing the accounts of the Altmark "incident." What an exploit!! But I will *not* discuss the war in this letter.

I must not forget your lovely calendar with its exquisite coloring. It has been much admired.

I sent you "Over On The Island" for our Xmas exchange and hope it escaped sinking.

I forget if I told you in my letter of last spring that "Anne of Windy Poplars" is to be in the movies. The R.K.O. is producing it now.

I'd really like very much to get a letter from you. I am lonely this winter. Chester is away in a home of his own,—Mr. Macdonald is spending the winter in Florida—and the nervous strain of world conditions is rather taking its toll of me as of everybody.

My letters from my friends are about all I have to help me keep up my morale.

I hope the photo I sent you at Xmas didn't get broken in transit. It is considered very "like" me.

Yours cordially
L. M. Macdonald

210A Riverside Drive
Toronto, Ont.

July 23/40

Dear Mr. MacMillan:

I was so relieved to get yesterday a copy of the Alloa Journal with your "Man In The Street" still forthcoming. I have been so worried about all those "Scotland raids" in the papers.

I am in rather bad shape. Seven weeks ago I fell and injured my right arm severely. It was not broken but the muscles and ligaments were so torn that I was completely helpless for four weeks and even yet, as you can see by my hand writing, it is very far from normal. I can write only a few words at a time with it.

It happened just when the war news was at its worst and the enforced inability together with the fact that I was run down and had several personal worries all combined to bring about a bad nervous breakdown. The last six weeks have been dreadful. I would rather die than live them again. The worst is a fixed idea that I will never be better though my doctor laughs at this & says all victims of neurasthenia believe this. This past week I have noticed a few faint symptoms of improvement. The awful and resultant restlessness seems not so bad. But I fear I have a long way to go ere I recover. When and if I do the sunshine of our friendship may shine again. If not please let me say again how much it has meant in my life.

Your parcels of John O'London's come at intervals. I have put them away to read sometime perhaps. I cannot read now. But please send them when you can. I do not ask you to write me until you hear I am better. All the things that once gave me pleasure bring only bitterness to me now. I feel turned into another personality.

I hope you can read this unintelligible scribble. The arm muscle is so weak I can't handle pen properly.

Yours as hopefully as possible
L. M. Macdonald

I may say Stuart graduated on June 6 and is now interning in a Toronto Hospital.

210A Riverside Drive

Aug. 27, 1940

Dear Mr. MacMillan:

You can never know what your sane letter, written along the old familiar lines, meant to me when it came a few days ago. I did not think such letters can be written nowadays. I suppose I am judging everyone from my own condition. Since my note to you of July 23 I had almost a month of intolerable distress. I seemed to be getting worse all the time. But ten days ago a change came. I really think I have turned the corner and my doctor says I have and will be all right in time. I realize I have a long way to go yet and it may be several months before I am able to answer your letter but I'll drop a card from time to time. The mere *hope* of getting well is so wonderful. For weeks I have been convinced I never could or would. My arm is much better and I can do many things without pain but some I can't yet. I can't write much at a time—a certain muscle gets very tired and I get [illegible] nervously.

I do hope you won't overwork yourself. I think it is fortunate your paper is so small. Do take care of yourself and don't disdain air raid shelters. When I couldn't sleep at night I would see you bombed and blown to pieces. My son Chester tried to join the Osgoode Hall Contingent but was turned down because of short sight. He is however in "Class B" and may have to go yet. Stuart graduated in medicine in June and is now interning in St. Michael's Hospital. By the decision of the Medical Council he cannot go or be called on till he finishes his intern year. Then—no one knows. But it was not the thought of this that caused my breakdown. Several things including my fall came all at once with the breaking of France and caused it. But now I really have some hope of recovering things do not look so black. But even yet I very often wonder what God can be thinking about!!!

Thank you for the heather. Its color was quite unfaded. And thank you for your letter.

Yours faithfully
L. M. Macdonald

POSTCARDS

[November 21, 1940]

Thanks for magazines. Am very ill. Still not able to write.

Yours as ever
L. M. Macdonald

February 28, [1941]

Dear Mr. M.:

I am no better and fear it will be a long time before I am. Yet the doctor claims I am. We are having a very cold rough winter.

Yours as ever
L. M. Macdonald

April 23, [1941]

Dear Mr. MacMillan:

Thanks for your cards and easter card to-day. The Easter has not yet come as I haven't had a good time and had a very bad year. I am thinking of your kindness in the kindness of never mentioning the horror. We have lived to see beauty vanished from the world.

Your old friend
L.M.M.

Aug. 26, 1941

Dear Friend:

Thanks for your letter and booklet. I do not feel any better and I cannot write letters or write at all only after I have had a hypo. I hope you will have a happy holiday.

Yours as of old
L. M. Macdonald

[Postcard]

Sept. 15, 1941

Am no better dear friend & never will be. You do not know the blows that have fallen on my life for years. I tried to hide them from my friends. I feel my mind is going.

Yours gratefully
L. M. Macdonald

Dec. 23, 1941

Dear Friend:
Thanks for your gift. I am no better and never will be. But I thank God for our long and beautiful friendship. Perhaps in some other incarnation in some other happier world we will renew it. This past year has been one of constant blows to me. My oldest son has made a mess of his life, and his wife has left him. My husband's nerves are worse than mine even. I have kept the nature of his attacks from you for over 20 years but they have broken me at last. I could not go out to select a book for you this year. Pardon me. I could not even write this if I had not had a hypodermic. The war situation kills me along with many other things. I expect conscription will come in and they will take my second son and then I will give up all effort to recover because I shall have nothing to live for.

May God bless you and keep you for many years. There are few things in my life I have prized as much as your friendship and letters. Remember me as I used to be, not as I am now.

Yours in all sincerity and perhaps
for the last time,
L. M. Macdonald

Epilogue

On April 24, 1942, four months after her last letter to MacMillan, L. M. Montgomery dies. She is taken back to Cavendish, where she lies in state in the house called "Green Gables," and is buried in the Cavendish cemetery. L. M. Montgomery had at last come home.

INDEX

206

tion, 24n.; comes to Cavendish, P.E.I., 24n.; secret engagement to Maud Montgomery, viii, 1, 24n., 57; studies in Scotland, 24; moves to Bloomfield, P.E.I., 37; moves to Leaskdale, Ontario, 57; wedding plans and marriage, 57-59, 68, 90; honeymoon, 1, 60-62, 65, 160n.; pastorate in Leaskdale, Ontario, 63; moves to Norval, 123, 127; retires to "Journey's End," 173-74; illnesses, viii, 63, 99, 106, 123, 168-73, 189-90, 193, 204

Macdonald, Hugh Alexander, 63, 71n.

MacDonald College, Montreal, Quebec, 95, 110

MacFarlane, Lieut. N. Cameron, 95n., 96

MacKenzie, Margaret (Woolner) [Aunt Margaret], 61

MacMillan, George Boyd, vii-xii, 1, 6n., 57n., 63, 78-79, 109-11, 123, 125, 160n., 173, 205

Macneill (family), v, vi, 2, 6, 183

Macneill, Alec, 153, 153n.

Macneill, Alexander Marquis, v, vi, 15, 45n.

Macneill, David, 182

Macneill, Hamilton, 183

Macneill, John Franklin, 56n., 89

Macneill, Reverend Leander, 24n., 51

Macneill, Lucy (Woolner), xi, xii, 15, 15n., 16, 52, 55-57, 61, 188-89

Macneill, Margaret, 182

Macneill, Mary Kennedy (Aunt May), 24, 24n., 25, 194

Macneill, May, 153, 153n.

Macneill, Myrtle (Mrs. Ernest Webb), 180, 180n., 182-83

Macneill, Pierce, 182-83

Magic for Marigold, 123, 140, 155, 164n.

Maine, U.S.A., 107, 121

Mammoth Cave, Kentucky, U.S.A., 120, 122

"Man In The Street," 200

Maritime Advocate, The, 190

Maritimes, 134, 186, 196

"Marmion," 58

Mars, 33, 86, 114

Mary, Queen of Scots, 140, 166

Massachusetts, 4-5, 45, 145

Master (Page lawsuit), 143, 145-46

Matthew (*Anne of Green Gables*), 179

McClures Magazine, 135

McDonald, Reverend Donald, 22n.

McIntyre, Bertie (Beatrice), 109n., 110-11, 120-21

McKenzies (family), 7

McLaren, Ian, 6

McLean, Lem, 150-51

McLeod, Angus, 159

McLeod, Skilly, 158-59

McRae, Mary Ann, 80n., 157

Megantic (ship), 59-60

"Memories," 78

Messenger, Gertrude, 179

Messenger of the Sacred Heart, The, 4

Milton, John, 113, 120

Milton, P.E.I., 150

"Minister's Wife, The," 137

Minter, Mary Miles, 153-54

Mistress Pat, 123, 177

Montgomery (family), 2, 7, 197

Montgomery, Alexander, 196-97

Montgomery, Clara Woolner (Macneill), v, 15, 55n., 182

Montgomery, Donald, 9-11

Montgomery, Senator Donald, 11, 11n., 197

Montgomery, Hugh, 9, 196

Montgomery Hugh Carlyle, 80n., 91

Montgomery, Hugh John, xi, 80n., 156-57, 159-60, 160n.

Montgomery, General John, 197

Montgomery, Lucy Maud: birth and family, xi, 15, 55n., 80n., 156-57, 159-60, 160n., 182; early childhood, xi, 15-16; spends year in Prince Albert, xi, 156; education, xi; teaches school, xi, xii; relationship with Herman Leard, xii, 1, 28-32; engagement to Edwin Simpson, 29-30; journalism, xii; origin of the correspondence, vii; physical description,